HOW TO DIRECT
THE HIGH SCHOOL PLAY

by

LEON C. MILLER

THE DRAMATIC PUBLISHING COMPANY

CHICAGO

© MCMLXVIII by

LEON C. MILLER

(HOW TO DIRECT THE HIGH SCHOOL PLAY)

TO FREDA

ACKNOWLEDGMENTS

The National Thespian Society for permission to use informative material collected over a period of years.

DRAMATICS, the official publication of The National Thespian Society, for permission to use certain copyright material.

"Jo" McKeown, my Girl Friday, for her helpful suggestions and recommendations and for typing the manuscript.

CONTENTS

FOREWORD . . . . Page 7

SELECTING THE PLAY . . . . Page 9

CASTING THE PLAY . . . . Page 14

REHEARSAL: INTERPRETATION AND
      CHARACTERIZATION . . . . Page 23

BLOCKING THE PLAY . . . . Page 35

TECHNICAL ORGANIZATION . . . . Page 46

PROJECTION . . . . Page 53

DRESS REHEARSALS . . . . Page 56

THE PERFORMANCE . . . . Page 60

AFTER GLOW . . . . Page 63

APPENDIX . . . . Page 65

FOREWORD

"Formal rules for staging and directing plays are made only to be broken." I heard this remark made by a director whose work was severely criticized at one of our Thespian stage conferences. In my personal judgment, his statement was purely defensive--an excuse for his own indifference or his own ignorance. Whenever a play is presented before an audience who paid to see it, that play, be it a short play, a full-length play, or a musical, must be as nearly professional as it is humanly possible to make it. Otherwise, there soon will be no audience left.

Thus my aims here are to help those who either with or without educational training wish successfully to stage and to direct plays for the public. These suggestions are directed particularly to high school teachers faced with the responsibility of directing their first or perhaps their twentieth play. Whether or not I am so qualified to author this text is a moot question except to say that I was a high school play director for over twenty years; and for the past seventeen years as executive secretary of The National Thespian Society, I have had the opportunity to witness productions of all kinds of high school plays under all sorts of conditions throughout the country.

Let me say here that standards of play production on the high school level have made phenomenal advances during the past ten to fifteen years. No longer are poorly written plays accepted by high schools; no longer will students, faculty, and community accept poorly staged and poorly directed plays. The class play directed by either the elected or appointed teacher with no training is rapidly disappearing from the American scene. In its place is the all-school play directed by one who has the know-how, whether through formal training or by just plain talent. Finally, publishers both large and small are now aware that only well-written plays with real-life situations will be accepted. The trashy plays that flooded the market years ago are now past history.

As I am limiting my subject to directing the play, emphasis on make-up, scenery, lighting, and costumes will not be stressed. There are excellent books on each of these subjects available. Little will be said about arena theatre, which I feel is only a substitute when a proscenium theatre is not practical. On the other hand, I shall try to cover all the areas from play selection to audience reception.

In conclusion, if I help through this medium even one high school play director to produce successfully his first play, or help him raise his own standards, then this book is worthwhile. There is no greater challenge nor more personal satisfaction than to present plays successfully before an appreciative audience.

LEON C. MILLER

Chapter One

SELECTING THE PLAY

Probably the most difficult task facing the inexperienced director is the choice of the play. Today it is not easy to find the right play. Twenty years ago plays were unsophisticated, easy to enact, usually one-set (the familiar living room set), and certainly uncomplicated in over-all general lighting. The commercial theatre was booming with plays, most of which were suitable for high school production. Non-commercial plays usually stressed teen-age problems, for then the consensus was that high school students could only interpret roles about their own school activities and about their own problems.

The high school faculty director was that unfortunate individual who was elected, due to popularity with the students, as class advisor. He might have been the physics teacher, the librarian, or the shop teacher. Thus with no educational training or experience in play directing, he had no other choice than to "put on" the class play. His choice of play was usually a poorly written non-royalty play with absurd themes. The important thing was not how well it was presented, but how much money could be raised for the yearbook or the annual class trip to Washington. As a result, these productions rightfully earned the ugly stigma, "high school play," which it has taken years to erase. In those days the audiences consisted only of parents and relatives of cast members, faculty, and possibly some of the student body. Yet with all of these bad features--poorly acted, badly directed, with inadequate scenery and lighting effects --these plays were always "the best ever produced," and they made money for the sponsoring class.

Today, it is a different story. School administrations have come to realize that theatre is an educational experience which requires specially trained teachers. They realize that theatre is not a "frill," but an important element in developing character, poise, good vocal habits and a general presence with crowds; that participation in drama is an education which is taken into adult living. In a number of schools there are theatre departments with qualified teachers who know their business. As a result, theatre today in our schools is much improved in selection and production. Although the stigma of yesterday is still around in some areas of our country, great strides forward have been made.

But the problem of finding better plays for production still exists. The commercial theatre has degenerated into an orgy of sex, adultery, racism, and narcotics--and furthermore, most of the straight plays on Broadway fold in several months. Granted, in the past several years we have had several good commercial plays; but quality plays are an exception rather than an annual occurrence. Thus most high schools must depend upon non-Broadway plays. Publishers of plays are aware of the problem and they are trying to solve it. However, the challenge for publishing good plays is not easy to meet.

In other days a publishing company could offer almost any kind of play with the assurance that it would have fair acceptance by our high schools. June Mad, Sixteen in August, and Seven Sisters are several titles of plays which were generally accepted by director, cast, and audience, with their light but well-intended themes. Today, however, the demand is for plays that have a real message, be it farce, comedy, or drama. The more recent successfully accepted plays, according to the annual National Thespian Society's survey, are The Mouse That Roared, Ask Any Girl, All Because of Agatha, Bull in a China Shop, Cheaper by the Dozen, Jenny Kissed Me, Tom Jones, Seventeenth Summer, and Everybody Loves Opal. Thus publishers, at a considerable financial gamble, are trying to meet the exacting demands of today's high school theatre.

What should a director look for in a play? First, he should be aware of faculty and community attitudes, he should know what he has in the way of staging and lighting facilities and student talent. High school theatre has special problems of its own. Let's start with faculty and community attitudes.

Whether or not we wish to accept it, the high school theatre is subjected to more severe censorship than any other theatre in the country. Therefore a director, old or new, must know what his community will allow on the stage--for what your community accepts, so will your administration. No two communities are alike. What can be done in one city may be taboo in another. Let me illustrate: Inherit the Wind has been censored, because it is too atheistic; as have Detective Story because of a suggestion of abortion, Junior Miss because of the language and a drunken hangover, Brick and the Rose because of narcotics. On the other hand certain high schools have produced Cat on a Hot Tin Roof; Look Back in Anger; You Can't Take It with You (without cutting); On Borrowed Time; Luther; Bell, Book, and Candle; Sabrina Fair; and The Seven Year Itch without any disastrous criticisms. So it is up to the director to make tactful inquiries among his colleagues and his fellow townspeople.

Too often a young, newly arrived university graduate in his first year at a teaching post feels he must raise the standards of the community by producing those plays he was in on the university campus. University plays usually are accepted without question on campus, but the same plays, based on sex, religion, or politics, can become the end of a promising directorial career and even result in the loss of a teaching position when produced on the high school stage.

One can raise standards without going overboard. Objectionable lines and scenes in most plays can be eliminated. There is no need for the drunken scene in You Can't Take It with You; swearing, smoking, and drinking can be easily eliminated in most plays and other substitutes offered. For example, one can drink tomato cocktails before dinner instead of martinis or Manhattans. If offensive lines, scenes, and actions cannot be changed or eliminated without killing the plot of the play, choose another play.

Although in many of the newer high schools one will find adequate stages, superb lighting facilities, dressing and make-up rooms, and scenery storage rooms, most high schools unfortunately are not so blessed. Thus the director in selecting his play must be sure that he has the space and the lights to do it well. Without fly space, plays with three or more changes of scenery must be passed by for one with simple sets. Scenery must be changed between scenes and acts within five minutes, or the whole play is in trouble. An audience loses its interest in the play if it has to sit for too long between scenes.

Small stages require plays with small casts. One cannot have beautiful stage pictures, or balance, on an overcrowded stage. To try to do The Remarkable Incident at Carson Corners with a cast of twenty-six on a so-called "2 by 4" stage is courting disaster. Rather, if such large-cast plays are your choice because you want everyone to get in the act, you had better do such plays in-the-round in your gymnasium.

One hesitates to recommend type casting, but whether we like it or not, certainly plays require just that. So, in making your final selection you must be sure, before there is any public announcement, that you have the students who can play the major roles. You must have a Sheridan Whiteside (The Man Who Came to Dinner), a Dino (Dino), an Elizabeth Barrett (Barretts of Wimpole Street), a grandpa Vanderhof (You Can't Take It with You), an Eileen (My Sister Eileen), a Marcellus (The Robe), and an Eliza, a Henry Higgins, and a Doolittle (Pygmalion) for a successful production. Remember, you have made your selection before your tryouts. If the talent is not there, again you are in deep trouble. This is an area where great care must be exercised. One does not stage a ballet unless he has dancers.

What kind of plays should be in a high school theatre program? There are the following categories: straight plays, children's theatre, and musicals. Depending upon the time available and the policy of the school, three full-length plays are recommended each year as follows: a comedy, a drama, and then either a children's theatre play or a full-length musical. Of course you may wish to do only one full-length play and the other two as mentioned. If such is the case, then your program should be planned on a two-year basis so that you offer comedy one year and drama the next. No greater harm can be done to any theatre program than to offer, let's say, three comedies each year.

To list plays recommended will take too much space. Thus I refer you elsewhere to the list of plays most often produced by National Thespian-affiliated schools during the past five years. In addition, the National Thespian Society has catalogues of both long and short plays in which you will find listings of all of the play publishers.

I do want to stress the value of doing children's theatre plays and also musical comedies. Too many schools shun plays for children because it is falsely assumed that such plays are too childish in their acting demands for high school students to perform. Nothing could be further from the truth. The most difficult play to present before a most critical audience is a children's theatre play. One has to be not good but superb, to hold the attention of grade schoolers for an hour or more with live theatre. Yet one will never feel nor meet a more appreciative audience for a play well done. They will not miss a trick, and they will never forgive you for long delays between scenes; but they will also be the audience that lives with you throughout every moment of the play. There is no greater challenge than performing a play for children!

Concerning musicals, I must remind you at the outset that they are very expensive to produce. High royalties, expensive orchestration rentals, elaborate scenery and costume costs must be anticipated. On the other hand, most musicals are well attended, even when performed four times. I have rarely heard of financial setbacks from doing musicals. However, you should not attempt doing a musical unless you have students who can sing the score and students who can dance. You, as director, need an instrumental musical director, a chorus director, and a good choreographer.

I have suffered through some high school musicals because the principals could not sing, the dances were atrocious, and the orchestra drowned out the soloists--and in some they even drowned out the choruses! Don't ever attempt a musical, Broadway or non-Broadway, unless the talent is there.

Finally, one gets exactly what he pays for--nothing more, nothing less. A poorly written non-royalty play is not worth the time and effort expended for production. Royalties are the least of your expenses. Authors and publishers must live, too. The better-known author means higher royalties for his plays. Pay it, for it is worth the small additional cost. If you are going to do a play at all, do a good one. You will find it easier to stage and much more rewarding both for the cast and for you, the director.

Chapter Two

CASTING THE PLAY

Once the play is selected, and once the director is familiar with all of the characters he needs, there then comes an extremely difficult assignment: discovering the right people for the right parts, be they major or minor. Here a mistake in casting can prove disastrous, not only for this one play, but for the entire theatre program at the school. The director must be sure his casting is as nearly perfect as it is humanly possible to make it. For once the cast is announced publicly, he has reached the point of no return. He has to stand by his decisions or else he is in for very real trouble with his administration, the student body, and the parent.

The director cannot even change the announced parts unless he is so requested by the individuals concerned, and then he can do it only with the approval of the entire cast. I recall one instance in which the leading role was given to a very intelligent girl, who had all the necessary qualifications and talent to fill the role. In the confines of the classroom in which tryouts were held, one physical defect went unnoticed--an extremely unpleasant smile due to large teeth. When the cast moved to the stage, her teeth became so noticeable that her beauty was lost under the cruel stage lighting. The director very unwisely removed her from the part--and then the brickbats began to fall. In the end the school was publicly criticized, and the play was a failure in performance and in attendance. Ultimately, the director was removed from her post, and a teenager's heart was very nearly broken. So, a high school play can become a very dangerous experience unless directors observe the rules of the game.

What then must one look for to be sure of his casting? Posture, voice, intelligence, reputation, willingness to cooperate, ability to work with others, industry, and the willingness to sacrifice personal ambitions in other fields--and a willingness and the ability to make time available for rehearsals.

Prior to tryouts the director must have the following information: <u>Names, homerooms in school, and home addresses of all students.</u>

The director must know beforehand approximately how many students will try out for the play so that adequate space can be made available, and so that there is enough time for everyone. Be sure to give yourself time and the opportunity to check further on each student. In my judgment, open tryouts are the best; in this way all of the hopefuls can see for themselves the talents of others. Thus when the final decisions are publicly announced, they will willingly accept them. High school students are fair-minded and can recognize their own shortcomings and the talents of others. It is also a good policy for the director to observe the reactions of a partisan audience to the talent that is displayed. I have seen such an audience warmly applaud the works of others, laugh heartily at comedy portrayals, and sometimes even brush away a tear or two during very dramatic portrayals.

The best place to hold tryouts is in the school auditorium. There are several reasons for this. First, there is adequate seating for all. Tryouts usually are long drawn-out affairs, and making students stand while they are waiting their turn both tires them and accentuates the agony. At tryouts, nerves are always on edge. The tensions are obvious, and emotions will run high. In addition, the students are literally battling stage fright. The right person may give up were he to feel that his comfort is ignored. It may be necessary to continue tryouts to a second or third day. A considerate director will, if such is the case, post the names of the students, listing the days they are to report. The time scheduled for tryouts should also be designated, as: 3:30 to 5:30 P.M. All students assigned to a specified day should try out on that day. To tell students, who have sat through two hours of tryouts, that they will have to return on the next day, is careless planning and unfair. It is much better to find you allotted too much time for the number trying out than to end a day's tryout before all of the students have been called.

Secondly, use the stage of the auditorium with the stage lights on. This gives you the opportunity to test voice quality, to observe poise, and to compare heights. Even your students will feel more at ease on the stage than in the front of a classroom. This will help them to lose some, if not all, of their self-consciousness and their feelings of inferiority. With the stage lights on, even a booth spotlight, they lose sight of their fellow students sitting in the auditorium. Most important, however, is that you get a better picture of the tryouts for the parts in the play. You will also have a much better idea of how they will appear before an audience on opening night because you saw them on stage when they first tried out.

If one wishes to reach students in school, the only place to find them is in their homerooms. A note for the student to the homeroom teacher is more satisfactory than a note to a teacher in class. There are some teachers who will not tolerate any disturbance of their class work--and <u>I think they are right.</u> Home addresses and telephone numbers are also going to be needed, for there are times when you will find it necessary to write the parents or to contact cast members at home.

PERSONALITY TRAITS

Although you, as the director, are in no position to tell any one student that he <u>cannot</u> try out for the play, you can easily eliminate him from further consideration if he does not measure up to your standards. This is done after he has completed his first tryout. Information concerning the following is essential: Scholarship, the student's other interests, his character and reputation, his previous experiences in theatre, and any recommendations of homeroom and classroom teachers.

SCHOLASTIC STANDING

You cannot risk selecting a student for even a minor role if he is a borderline student, no matter how much talent he may seem to have. Granted, in athletics, students' grades are sometimes overlooked because the coach may need the beef and the brawn; but this is not so in dramatics. A student who is careless with his homework and who has an inability to apply himself in the classroom is a very poor risk for even a minor part in a play. In nine out of ten cases, this same attitude of indifference or inability, or both, will carry over into rehearsals and the performance. The play can quickly become an excuse for even poorer grades. Homework will be an excuse for not memorizing lines on time. And this individual always has friends who make him late for rehearsals. Finally, his indifference and shortcomings will soon turn to criticism of you as director and of his fellow cast members as actors. Then he will start to carry bad reports about the play. He may even walk out on you at any one of your rehearsals. So leave the poor student alone. Parts in the play are for the good students and the workers. Secondly, you must have the cooperation of your fellow teachers. One of the easiest ways I know to lose just that is to cast a poor student in a major role. You need the help of your fellow teachers on many occasions, as they will chair your student committees. So you must accept their opinions about any student whose class work is shaky. Doing it any other way is too much of a gamble. There are enough pitfalls in theatre already.

OTHER INTERESTS

I have found that the person you want in the cast is usually among the busiest students in school. These people are in orchestras and choruses, on the staffs of the Annual or the school newspaper, and are members of student councils and officers in school clubs. But be sure, <u>be very sure</u>, that such a student is going to be free for rehearsals. This is especially important if he is cast in a major role. A written statement from him before tryouts that he will be available whenever you need him is a <u>must</u>. The morale of your entire cast will be shaken, if not destroyed, if the rehearsal must stop until the tardy student arrives. Here again you have to deal with consultation with other faculty members. If you are considering such a busy student for a role, you should have the approval of his faculty advisor before he is publicly cast. Granted, his other interests are important; but if these interests cannot be laid aside during rehearsals, you will antagonize other members of the faculty and the members of your cast, and you will intensify your own frustrations. It is not worth it, if satisfactory arrangements cannot be worked out for all concerned, to cast such a busy student.

CHARACTER AND REPUTATION

As the character of the student is covered under the heading of Scholastic Standing, these paragraphs will stress reputation. You need the help of your Guidance Directors, faculty class sponsors, and homeroom teachers to determine whether or not the students are of good repute. Students themselves will be of little aid, for they will not become stool-pigeons--and rightly so. Here we deal with the question of morals, absences from school, associates, and the students' habitats. Students with poor morals, regardless of talent, should not be accepted in romantic plays. Even a brief stage kiss will bring laughter from your student audiences, for they well know the principles involved. If the theme is based morally on choosing between what is right or what is wrong, as in <u>Seventeenth Summer</u>, the effectiveness of the play will be lost, for your young actors in their everyday living may have already made the wrong choice. Sometimes penny-throwing onto the stage during romantic scenes can occur; this is simply the reaction of the audience to your bad choice of leads.

Students caught being absent from school without leave have no place in your cast. The chances are that your administration will not permit you to select them for, in a way, by such selection you are either ignoring this evil or placing your stamp of approval on such misconduct. Furthermore, if he plays hooky from school, what is to stop him from playing hooky from rehearsals?

You should learn about the conduct of all the students in their home rooms, classes, study halls, and in other allied activities. Are they ever discipline problems, are they discourteous or uncooperative? How well are they regarded by the other students? Do they have many friends? Are they popular? Do they work with others satisfactorily even in minor assignments? Are they argumentative? Do they accept orders in a reasonable way? These questions need to be asked.

How well do they dress; how do they wear their hair--I could go on and on. And finally, where do your prospective cast members spend their time when they are out of school? In other days, poolrooms and dance halls were out-of-bounds. Today there are other public places, whatever they are called, where high school students have no reason for being.

All of these factors are important, for your play must not be cast with the misfits, the unintelligent, the odd ones, or the outlanders. Directors are not psychologists, and plays must not be used as a treatment for those who are unbalanced in one way or another. You must not attempt to present a play to a paid audience with a cast of students (one or several) who do not have the mental ability to do characterizations or to memorize lines, and who are unstable in everyday living, whether it is in the school or in the community at large.

WRITTEN PERMISSION FROM PARENTS

Although I shall stress later on other correspondence with parents, I feel that each student should present to the director a written permission from parents to try out for the play. The importance of this lies in the fact that the parents then know their teen-agers are trying out. Parents need to know that preparing a play is time-consuming, hard work, and that their sons and daughters are tackling another difficult assignment in addition to their regular class work. Make it clear that the cast members will not be available for work either at home nor at a job in the after-school hours. The director, by requesting this permission and making the obligation clear at the beginning, is only protecting himself should some questions arise later.

TRYOUT METHODS

There are several generally recognized and accepted methods for casting. You can use creative dramatics or prepared auditions, or you can have readings from the play that you are planning on giving. In the last case, scripts should be made available at least a month before the tryouts. Or you can have a "cold" reading of the script. Of these four, the first two are preferred for casting the play.

When I cast my plays, the first thing I asked the student to do was to create a character in a situation. For example, he could be reacting to a knock on the door during a thunderstorm. Other possible situations might be: hearing noises downstairs after retiring, greeting a husband on leave from the Army, having the telephone ring when you know that prowlers are about, baby-sitting with an obstreperous six-year-old. You can add to this list so that you have interpretations of romance, fear, and comedy. Let me add a word of warning: Do not reduce your creative suggestions to the ridiculous, such as a bear on the prowl. The situations should suggest a real-life experience.

Having satisfied myself that the student can think quickly on his feet, then my next step is to permit him to render his prepared, well-memorized monologue. Notice I used the word monologue, for no two students should ever try out together. It is not fair, for one part is always stronger than the other, not unlike the straight man and the comedian. As he delivers his monologue, I would move about the auditorium in order to study the quality of his voice, his posture, his gestures, his facial expressions. It is not necessary to hear and see the entire monologue--three minutes is all that you need to determine whether or not he has what you are looking for. From both his creativity and his prepared audition you can now do one of two things: drop him, or mark your card for the role you think best fits him.

Having scripts available prior to tryouts in my judgment belongs in colleges and universities--not in the high school. In the first place, this method may discourage students rather than encourage them to try out. They may conclude that they do not fit into any of the parts. Thus you may have lost the right person for the right part. Secondly, it can encourage them to try out for certain parts which they do not fit at all. Then if they are selected for some other roles, they are bewildered and confused, for that is not what they tried out for. They might even reject the parts you give them. High school students are very sensitive.

Reading "cold" from the script is the worst method of all. Most high school students cannot do that without help. By merely having them read from the play, you have limited yourself to a judgment of their voices and possibly an interpretation of a part. I would want to see more than that before I made my selections. There are also, I have found, some students who are poor readers but superb actors after they have had time to memorize and work up a part.

Do not call students back for a second tryout. If you do, the problem is that you raise hopes all along the line. Thus the disappointment is magnified when those who do not get cast learn the bad news. On the other hand, I would call back all of those trying out, especially if it took several days, in order to check stage groupings. You know what your cast is going to be, but now you can check heights. By placing the entire group on the stage, you can move all of them about without revealing the final results of the tryouts or offering further encouragement.

A word or two is necessary regarding appearances Your leads must go well together--really your entire cast must make an attractive appearance even if they do not all get together until the curtain call. This final check is all you need to verify your final selections.

THE PUBLIC ANNOUNCEMENT OF THE CAST

If in your school you still hold general assembiles, here is the spot to announce the cast. Reading names and then having the students come on stage will soon become a standard accepted by your student body. They will realize that play casts are honored students. Also, this is an excellent way to start your publicity. Believe me, such public recognition offers a real challenge to those students who are cast in subsequent plays. Your entire theatre program will soon become second to none of all your school activities.

If general assemblies are no longer held in your school, then use the school newspaper to announce the cast. Here again you are using a public communication, read by all; thus you again add prestige to your whole program. I have seen the rush for copies of the paper as they were delivered to the homerooms--not just by the students who tried out, but by all the students. On the other hand, the use of out-of-school newspapers is not recommended, for in most cases your announcement will be buried deep on the inside pages Keep this important announcement within the school proper. The community newspapers should be used later for publicity.

Finally, if neither of the two methods mentioned above is feasible, then use the public address system of the school while the students are still in their home rooms. Do not do this during class time, for no teacher wants his class work disrupted by such an important announcement. If the time and talent are available, this program can be made really worthwhile and exciting by using some background music, sound effects, and a few clever introductory lines.

The important lesson to learn here is that the announcement of the cast must be done publicly. Do not keep this information secret. The students should learn who made the cast from their fellow students. You want to arouse interest in the play so that you will have sizable audiences on the evenings of the performances. And a fine way to start your publicity is by publicly announcing your cast. Let the students who worked so hard to make the grade be honored.

So far, we have stressed qualifications for casting straight plays. Now, what about casting for children's theatre and musicals? Is there any difference? Practically none. However, in casting children's plays, I would lay more stress at tryouts on creativity. Here you must find students who can play animal parts, as in Winnie-the-Pooh, The Land of the Dragon, Little Red Riding Hood, Mr. Popper's Penguins, The Wind in the Willows, and The Three Bears, and parts of Indians, princesses and pirates found in plays like Peter Pan, Wizard of Oz, Pinocchio, Rumpelstiltskin and Aladdin. These roles are far more difficult to master than those in other plays. Your student body's attitude toward plays for children is very important. You may have to do some spadework before casting this kind of play--but it is certainly worth a try.

If you're going to do a musical, there are several additional requirements. First, do you have students who can really sing and dance? Are you qualified, as some directors are. to originate dance numbers? If not, is there such a qualified person on your faculty or in your community? Granted, some of the more intricate dance numbers can be eliminated, but not all of them. When people come to see musicals, they expect to see dancing and to hear singing. Here I would make the music available so that the lead soloists sing those numbers you are actually going to do, and only do those numbers at the tryouts. You can then judge voice range, ability to project the songs over an orchestra, and the ability to interpret the songs with the acting. Be sure to announce what kind of dancers you need: ballet, tap, soft-shoe, line dancing; and then see to it the dances are so done. A musical comedy, be it Broadway or non-Broadway, is not a variety show. It is a play with music, which requires excellent acting, superb singing and dancing. Anything less than that will prove disastrous.

Now what about those students who are not cast in the play? Are they to be ignored, or dropped, as if they were not up to your standards? No. Nothing could be worse for your theatre program. In some cases, explanations may be in order. Perhaps they need more voice training, or their physical appearance is wrong for the show. Further hope should be offered, <u>if you honestly believe so</u>, that the next play may have the roles they can portray. Then you should encourage them to participate in your backstage crews.

You are going to need prop, scenery, lighting, costuming, make-up, and publicity crews. So hold their interest and enthusiasm for of "such stuff are good theatre programs made." They want to be a part of your theatre program, for there their interest lies. You're going to need them for a continuing theatre program for years ahead if you want that program to be successful.

In conclusion, finding the <u>right</u> person for the <u>right</u> part as the second step for the presentation of a successful play is a real challenge. With the public announcement of your cast you are indicating that you have found a Marcellus, a Dino, an Eliza, or a Mr. Higgins. You are telling your school and your community that all other parts are satisfactorily filled, that you will present a production worthy for them to <u>pay</u> to see. Don't let them down!

Chapter Three

REHEARSAL:
INTERPRETATION AND CHARACTERIZATION

In the commercial theatre, and possibly in the university theatre, the director takes a great deal of preliminary time (often as much as a year) preparing himself for his forthcoming chores. He thus can devote as much time as he needs to studying the play as a whole--the author's message, the roles, the words to be accented in each speech, the tempo or beat of the scenes, stage movements, blocking, and the preparation of his prompt book. No high school director is so blessed. He is too busy with his other daily chores.

The critics of the high school theatre--and adverse criticisms seem to be a national pastime, especially by faculty members of our universities--are unaware of the environments in which high school play directors work. They are unaware of or ignore the fact that directors are high school teachers--teachers who are carrying a full teaching load five days of the week. In addition to classes, they serve as proctors of study halls, and have home room responsibilities. Also, there are homework to look over, papers to correct and a lot of bookkeeping work on class attendance, grade records to be kept, and, finally, preparation of the teacher's daily lesson plans. It is amazing that the quality of high school plays has made such remarkable progress under such adverse working conditions.

Very few directors select their plays for each current year until schools open in the fall, for the majority wait for the latest releases, and they need some idea of who is going to be in the class. They look forward to receiving the new catalogues from the publishers. Then comes the purchase of reading copies which may or may not result in finding the right play. Even a newly released play that is an excellent one takes from two to three years to reach its deserved status in the Thespian Annual Survey. As an example, The Mouse That Roared took two years to reach the number one spot; The Curious Savage took three years. It is likewise very obvious that many plays released years ago still remain favorites since they coninue year after year among the top ten in the survey. Our Town, You Can't Take It with You, The Night of January 16th, and Our Hearts Were Young and Gay are some of these plays.

It is thus apparent that in high school plays, casting and rehearsals follow almost immediately after the play is selected. The director depends upon stage directions, usually inadequate, which are found in the playbook. Interpretation of lines has to be worked out as rehearsals progress, and characterizations usually come after lines are memorized. The prompt book becomes his bible as it is scored during rehearsals.

However, there is no excuse for a poorly directed play. The responsibility for a finished performance is that of the director. Whether or not he likes it, he must find time to study the play, to study the lines, and to be fully informed about the characterizations called for. He has no other choice unless he is willing to relinquish his post. A play director rarely resigns, for once bitten by the theatre bug, he is usually "hooked." Directing is a habit hard to break.

So the director calls the first meeting of his cast. Here playbooks are distributed, roles assigned, and the first reading begins. I see no sense in a brief synopsis of the play being given until after the reading is completed. The only prior instruction necessary at this time is to mark exits and entrances, stage movements, and gestures as suggested by the author. After the entire play is read, then, with no comments from the director, the students should discuss the purpose of the play--the aims of the author. Is it comedy or farce? Is it drama or melodrama? Is it a love story, a period play, a mystery? Is its primary theme emotion or suspense, is it pointing a moral, or is it a satire? Is it a realistic play or the theatre of the absurd? Has the author presented true-to-life situations?

Now comes the homework for the cast. There are three assignments for them. They should learn the history of the play; then they must study their lines, especially certain words, as they reach out for an interpretation; and they have to study the characterizations. The cast should have from three to five days to complete the assignment before you call your second meeting.

HISTORY OF THE PLAY

Whether it is a modern or a period piece, each play has a history. If it is adapted from a short story or a novel, this original source should not just be read but studied. If it is a Broadway play, the reviews by the critics should be scrutinized carefully. Why was the play favorably accepted or rejected? Believe it or not, the critics' reactions to Broadway plays are usually right, the only two exceptions to the best of my knowledge being for Abie's Irish Rose and Tobacco Road. However, a box office failure on Broadway, even when it has favorable reviews, will not necessarily be a financial failure in the high school field, as is best illustrated by The Curious Savage. Further research in DRAMATICS, a magazine published by the National Thespian Society, will reveal productions by other high schools and open up the possibility of correspondence with these schools. The more you know about the play and the author, the better will be the interpretations and the characterizations.

Period plays, such as Pride and Prejudice, Tom Jones, The Robe, The Miser, The Doctor in Spite of Himself, and Everyman, require even further research. Now one must study the times in which the character lived, the political environment, the foibles of the day, the moral problems and, in some cases, the religion. A true perspective of the times in which those people lived is essential in order to understand their manners and moods. Even the costumes they wore and the accessories accompanying their dress, such as rapiers, hidden daggers, handkerchiefs, scarfs, are a part of the homework. It is not an easy task for teen-agers to live the lives of characters of the Civil War or of the Elizabethan era without doing this background work.

ACCENTING LINES

A more difficult task for your cast is to read lines as the author intended them to be read. The primary task here is the ability to recognize the words that need to be stressed in each sentence. One simple illustration follows:
1. <u>Let</u> <u>me</u> <u>go</u>--suggests determination to resist.
2. Let <u>me</u> go--willingness.
3. Let me <u>go</u>--surprise.
4. <u>Let</u> me go--hope that such will not happen.

A director is usually surprised to find how well his young cast can interpret lines provided he has checked on their scholarship abilities before casting. This is the first step taken by a student in projecting his own ability, understanding, and talent. It should not be curbed, but encouraged.

CHARACTERIZATIONS

Here the results of the homework will be noticeable and, I am afraid, unsatisfactory. Bold as high school students seem to be as observed in their everyday living--jubilant at successful achievement, weeping at failures, explosive at times--they are really more timid and reserved, especially when alone--and they are just that at the first several rehearsals. Thus rarely does "the ham" show itself, or the inner emotion appear in the daylight. Thus the director will best find out the results of the homework by asking questions. How old is the character? Is he timid or bold? Is he basically honest or dishonest? Is he selfish? Is he considerate of others or is he self-centered? Ambitious or lazy? A bully? Cruel? Mentally sound? Do you know anyone like him among your schoolmates? Among adults, as: the shopkeeper, the policeman, the teacher, your relatives? The answers to these questions will give to the director some idea of the task which lies before him as he works to mold the students to their roles.

You are now ready for the second and final reading of the play. If the cast have done their homework well, there will be a marked improvement over the first reading. If lines are not interpreted as they should be, this is the time to make corrections--not the final, for progress in interpretation continues throughout the first several weeks of rehearsals. Little can be done about characterizations, for this is merely a reading, not an acting demonstration. Orders now are issued for the memorization of lines. A time schedule should be set up by acts; that is, the books must be out of their hands by a set date--and you must mean exactly that. However, the director cannot be unreasonable with his schedule. Acts cannot be memorized overnight. Besides, there are at least two more rehearsals which will be necessary before the playbooks can be discarded.

REHEARSALS

Successful rehearsals run for a period of six weeks--and casts need that much time for high school plays. You are going to need to set up a time schedule by scenes and acts, and you will need a place for rehearsals; also written notices will need to be sent off to parents; and a student secretary, a prompter, and a student director will have to be selected.

TIME SCHEDULES

Each member of the cast must receive a time and place schedule, such as the one shown on page 27, for each rehearsal. In addition, this schedule must be broken down in such a way that those in minor roles do not have to sit through nearly the entire act just to make an entrance as a maid or to say two or three lines.

The schedule should cover the entire six weeks, including the evening dress rehearsals during the final week. Now there is no excuse for any member of the cast to be tardy, for he has the schedule in black and white. In item number 4 on Oct. 2, notice that the minor

	DATE	PLACE	TIME	REHEARSAL	CAST
1.	Oct. 1	Auditorium	3:30-5:30	Act I	Principals
2.	Oct. 1	Auditorium	4:30	Act I	Maid, Policeman
3.	Oct. 2	Room 221	3:30-5:50	Act I	Principals
4.	Oct. 2	Room 221	3:30	Act I	Maid, Policeman
5.	Oct. 3	Auditorium	3:30-5:30	Act I	Entire Cast

roles report at the start of the rehearsal, which means that their parts will be taken first. It is only fair to schedule rehearsals in this manner so the minor roles don't have to sit through rehearsal after rehearsal until the very end. Let them rehearse first on a number of occasions and then let them go.

NOTICES TO PARENTS

This is where those home addresses come in handy. The time schedule of rehearsals must be mailed, <u>not sent home by cast members,</u> to all parents so that they are fully informed of the whereabouts of their children. They can plan their evening meals accordingly, and during the week of evening rehearsals they will know at just what time to expect the students home. Parents will appreciate this gesture. Likewise, it takes the director "off the hook" if the members of his cast are tardy in reaching home. A word of warning: This schedule should be observed to the letter, even though one may very much want to "finish the act." When the scheduled time for dismissal has arrived, let the students go.

SELECTION OF STUDENT SECRETARY

A director needs a secretary at each rehearsal to carry the director's prompt book. Then as rehearsals progress and as hand props are inserted and as changes are made in gestures and movements, the student secretary will make note of these in the director's prompt book. A good director, from the very start of rehearsals, will never have a playbook in his hands. He should be too busy watching, listening, and placing his cast--in other words, directing. The student secretary must receive recognition in the printed program of the play.

SELECTION OF PROMPTER

As soon as books are discarded, the student prompter goes to work. All directors know that lines, apparently perfectly memorized, are occasionally forgotten at the first several rehearsals of each act. The prompter keeps the play moving. On the other hand, the job of the prompter is finished by the time dress rehearsals are reached, <u>for there should be no prompting on the evenings of the actual performance.</u> Your cast must be informed that they are on their own. Another job of the prompter is to call to the attention of the director any mutation of lines, so that the cast can be so warned that lines must be memorized letter perfect. The prompter, too, must be rewarded by having his name in the printed program.

STUDENT DIRECTOR

Although some high school directors may not agree with me, I firmly believe that student directors should not be used to direct any high school play to be presented publicly to a paying audience. They are not mature enough to understand interpretation, characterization, blocking, scenery, and lighting; and furthermore, they lack the necessary educational training and experience. Your audiences expect the best, and only an experienced faculty director can offer a finished performance.

On the other hand, a student to take charge of, but not direct, a rehearsal must be available at all times. It will be his sole responsibility to start the rehearsal and to keep it moving when the director is delayed by more urgent business. With his presence, rehearsals will not bog down because of interruptions. He, too, should be so recognized in the program.

Students should be encouraged to direct plays, however--plays to be presented publicly before audiences who do not pay admission. This is excellent training for leadership and worthwhile experience in working with others. Either on the program or by public announcement, there should be a statement that the plays were student-directed.

The next two rehearsals are, as I call it, walking through the entire play. A classroom will not be satisfactory because of its limited acting space; your auditorium stage-- where the play will be finally presented--is the only satisfactory place. Set the stage first by using chairs or other available furniture for your sofa, tables, chairs, etc. as outlined in the playbook. Indicate where the fireplace will be, the telephone, the table lamps, the window. Point out the exits, outside, interior, hallway, stairs, etc. Now, with books in hand, the reading and the walking begin. You, the director, should be seriously studying the movements. Your secretary or book-holder stops the action if a member of the cast moves incorrectly either upstage or downstage, left or right. Notice the different areas of the stage shown on the diagram on page 31. Give the author a chance before you decide you do not like this movement or stage position. Before long, however, you find the stage directions inadequate so you will have to take over--not at this rehearsal but at the next, after you have made notes for the re-blocking of certain scenes. Blocking becomes one of the first of your many home assignments. By the way, the director is not interested in interpretation or characterization at these "walk-on" rehearsals, only on stage movements and stage pictures. You will find that Broadway plays usually have the most confusing stage directions. Any director who has done Arsenic and Old Lace, You Can't Take It with You, or The Man Who Came to Dinner knows what I am talking about. Your cast may realize you are as bewildered as they are about certain movements. Admit it--with the promise, however, that by the next rehearsal you will have the problem solved. It may be the wee hours of the morning before you find a satisfactory solution; but such is the price paid to be a director.

Rehearsals follow rehearsals for the next five weeks. Now comes the real task of characterization. A director will have to show to his cast how to walk, how to sit down in a chair gracefully, what gestures to use, how to hold a girl in one's arms, how to act the age of the character. He cannot do these things by sitting down in the rear of the auditorium; he will have to go on stage and act the part himself for all to see. Yet, he must be careful that what he does is not simply aped by the student, that the gesture shown is comfortable to the actor as well as all other movements. He must be sure that the characterization is natural, not forced, not "over-acting" but real to life.

In most plays there are scenes in which only two characters, usually the leads, appear. To further characterization, private rehearsals should be scheduled for these scenes, best illustrated in East of Eden and The Barretts of Wimpole Street. These rehearsals can be scheduled during free periods in school (if one is lucky to find his principals both have study hall at the same time) or at the director's home in the evenings. Nothing bogs down an afternoon rehearsal more than to have all the cast members in attendance and then have the director spend minutes to an hour working only with his two principals. Enthusiasm for the play decreases anyway after several weeks of rehearsal, though it will return as you approach dress rehearsals. Don't add to this problem by long, tedious rehearsals where you spend too much time on the principals in their duo-acting roles while you neglect the remainder of the cast.

MUSICALS AND CHILDREN'S THEATRE

Too often in musicals and in children's theatre, the interpretation of the parts and developing characterizations are ignored as everyone focuses on the glamor of the songs, the costumes, and elaborate scenery. Granted, this glamor and color sometimes can cover up weak spots in the production which would be very noticeable in straight plays; still, these cannot be excuses for poor directing. First, let's take

CHART OF STAGE POSITIONS

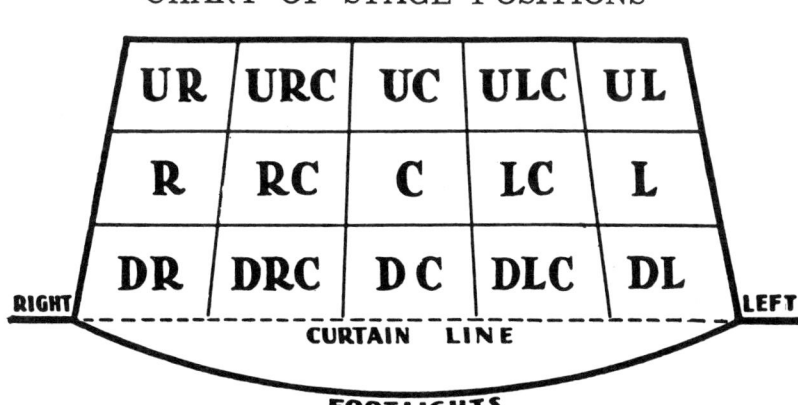

STAGE POSITIONS

Upstage means away from the footlights, *downstage* means toward the footlights, and *right* and *left* are used with reference to the actor as he faces the audience. R means *right*, L means *left*, U means *up*, D means *down*, C means *center*, and these abbreviations are used in combination, as: U R for *up right*, R C for *right center*, D L C for *down left center*, etc. A territory designated on the stage refers to a general area, rather than to a given point.

NOTE: Before starting rehearsals, chalk off your stage or rehearsal space as indicated above in the *Chart of Stage Positions*. Then teach your actors the meanings and positions of these fundamental terms of stage movement by having them walk from one position to another until they are familiar with them. The use of these abbreviated terms in directing the play saves time, speeds up rehearsals, and reduces the amount of explanation the director has to give to his actors.

musicals.

Too often a person is cast in musicals because of the quality of his voice, without paying proper attention to his ability to act. Both are essential. No musical should be attempted, as I mentioned earlier, unless you have high school students who can sing well, interpret roles superbly, and have the talent for the characterizations that are called for. Songs must be interpreted just as parts are, and the actor must remain in character while he is singing. Often a spotlight is thrown on the actor--and he stands before the audience singing a solo as if he were at a recital or at a church service. The whole show stops dead in its tracks. Both the cast and the audience are penalized, for at the conclusion of the number the thread of the story must be picked up. When this happens too often, the show drags, the audience tires--and the whole production becomes much too long.

There is a tendency for high school audiences to applaud the singing of each song and the outstanding dance numbers. Welcome as applause is to all of us, the evil here is that these interruptions destroy characterizations for bows--or, more unfortunately, for encores. Let the applause ring in their ears, BUT DO NOT STOP THE ACTION OF THE SHOW. Your young actors must remain in character from the opening of the curtain to its close. Encores are in order only when they are found in the original script and directions. When Mary Martin sang the show-stopping number, "Hello Dolly," in the show of the same name, which I was fortunate to see, she stayed in character--as did the remainder of the cast--throughout the tremendous applause, and then, moments later, went into an encore as written in the show. At the conclusion of the encore the applause was stilled by the progressing of the show. Remember, the show must go on, your actors remain in character, no matter what reactions occur in the audience.

Remember that the dance numbers are not variety show acts. Your dancers are characters in your play and must hold their characterizations throughout the entire routines. If the dance is somber, as in West Side Story, your dancers must create this atmosphere; if joyous, as in Bye Bye Birdie, the characterizations are happy, smiling actors in the environment of the play. No dance number should look as if it is work, a difficult task in which the participants are unsure of the next routine. All dance numbers must be professionally performed in order to hold characterizations. For the good of the show, it is far better to eliminate dance numbers which cannot be done well, no matter how difficult it may be for those students who have to be dropped. For your chorus numbers, the same rules apply as for the dance routines.

CHILDREN'S THEATRE

As high school students portray roles in plays for children, there are tendencies to emote to such an extent that the roles become exaggerated, or even ridiculous, and thus unacceptable by young children. Animals must remain animals throughout the entire performance--never become human beings merely portraying rabbits, penguins, birds, mice, or wolves. Probably the most difficult job of the director is to destroy the feeling of self-consciousness in playing animal roles. Some students will feel silly and embarrassed in animal parts; others will be so sincere that they will destroy the illusions by "hamming" the roles. The difficult period for characterization is the rehearsal which calls for such animal portrayals in everyday school clothes. When the actors are in costume this problem usually solves itself.

Characterizations other than that of animals, such as Pinocchio, Little Red Riding Hood, and Aladdin, follow the same rules as all plays. Have the actors read the original source of the play and study all of the possible interpretations and finally feel the part inwardly. A director must be very careful in his observance that the cast is not playing down to the youthful audience, but rather up to them. The children know the story being dramatized; sometimes they know it better than the members of the cast. They have even played these roles in their own imagination. They are not going to accept anything but the best.

Finally, there are two theories of acting: One is that the student must become so engrossed in the role that he loses his own identity, that he is the person he is portraying; the other, that no matter how deeply the actor feels the part, he never for one moment loses sight of the fact that he is acting. Of the two I prefer the second. I want my young actors to feel their roles, to laugh sincerely at that which is funny, to weep real tears at that which is sad--but not to such an extent that they forget rehearsed stage movements, recommended gestures, and the exits and entrances. I want them to pick up that which is accidentally dropped on stage rather than to continue to walk around it again and again until the audience reacts unfavorably to this distraction. Any student who takes liberties not rehearsed during the actual performance, who adlibs or drops cue lines simply because he is totally lost in the role, should be strongly reprimanded no matter how well he plays his part. His "lost identity" may so upset the other members of the cast that the over-all performance may suffer. The director must sense such inclinations or temperaments during rehearsals and curb them as they occur. It is a good procedure to remind the cast occasionally that they are "acting."

Sometimes during rehearsals the director will wonder why he selected this play, why he cast this student in this role. He will be sure the play is going to be a "turkey." He will swear up and down that after this play is over, he is through--never ever will he direct another play. This mood comes to everyone. It is as much a part of the play as opening night. Yet slowly, very slowly, the play begins to shape up. The characterizations start to come through. The lines begin to sparkle. Now he will even be looking forward to that final week of dress rehearsals.

The director now finds that he does not have to go on stage any more. He can move about the auditorium to listen and to see. The interruptions to correct enunciation, pronunciation, projection--to change stage movements, postures, gestures become less frequent. He can concentrate on the whole stage picture rather than on one or two characters. He becomes aware of the tempo, the <u>beat</u>, <u>beat</u>, <u>beat</u> of the action. He is almost ready for his audience, but not quite, for there remains ahead a sometimes frustrating week of dress rehearsals.

Chapter Four

BLOCKING THE PLAY

The director now has his own homework. He has to block the play so that throughout the entire performance his casts present delightful and charming stage pictures that also help to tell the story and set the mood of the scene or the act. This task starts with preliminary planning before the first rehearsal is called and ends at the first complete dress rehearsal. No matter how well the plans seem at first study, difficult problems will arise at rehearsals as your young actors start to move about the stage.

PRELIMINARY BLOCKING

First, on a large flat piece of white cardboard draw the stage set as found in the play itself. The arches, doors, windows, fireplaces, stairs, and other essentials must be included. Next, you place all furniture--sofas, tables, chairs, bookcases, light stands, and end tables--where they belong as is suggested in the script. Now you place on the furniture the suggested properties; e.g., putting lamps on end tables. Doll furniture is particularly useful for this planning.

Finally, see how well you can light your stage with available spotlights. If your stage is equipped only with the now obsolete border lights and footlights, you have very little choice for effective lighting.

The second step is to acquire either small blocks, checkers, or chess pieces to be your characters. Label each one--and you need one for each character--with the name of the character, not the name of the student playing the role. These characters you move about your stage as directed by the text. With this set-up you are nearly ready to start blocking the play, for you have followed the original directions of the author.

Would that it were smooth sailing from here on out! However, one quickly becomes aware of his own physical limitations as he studies the set. First, are you using flats or curtains for your interior scenes? If there are several scenes, do you have ample space to do this by using an interior draw curtain? If there are changes of scenery, either interior or exterior, do you have ample space and time for the rapid change?

Wide stages, not deep stages, create as many problems as those found on small stages. You are aware, either from your educational training or from experience, that for straight plays you cannot use the whole width of a wide stage, for your cast would need roller skates to cross on cue from one side to the other. Thus you reduce the width of your stage by using the front curtain to mask in the set, whether you are masking flats or a cyclorama. A careful director will be aware of the following:

1. Set should be approximately one foot behind the front curtain to allow enough clearance.
2. Wings will be used on the left and right front to mask out backstage areas. (Diagram A)
3. The tow rope of the front curtain should be marked so that it is never opened beyond the extension of the wings.
4. Sight lines can be tried out by sitting in auditorium seats down front on the far right and the far left to be sure that the entire acting area is visible. If sight lines do suffer, then those auditorium seats with obstructed vision must not be sold. (Diagram A)
5. Spotlights can be moved and adjusted to light properly all acting areas.
6. Depth of set is usually no problem on large stages. Yet, there are high school stages too wide, but with too little depth. In this case, center exits must be eliminated. Your blocking will now become a problem, for all directions for center entrances and exits must be re-blocked to side entrances.

Small stages, neither wide nor deep, are real problems. With such stages you are limited in your choice of play and cast size. The chances are the director will have to do almost all of the blocking for the whole play because the directions in the text will not fit. The only aid in such circumstances is to stress again the use of the front curtain as a wing and to be doubly sure that backstage areas cannot be seen at any time by the audience.

Further study of your completed drawing of the set may reveal other problems. For example, the set cannot be matched by your scenery. Let us suppose a fireplace must be in the down left wall, but the script of the play indicates it is to be up right. Windows and doors are often changed. Or a stairway may be built to go up left to center across the stage as is called for in <u>Arsenic and Old Lace</u>, but your stairway must be up right and across the stage. As I mentioned above, a shallow stage depth does not permit center exits or entrances. So, re-blocking

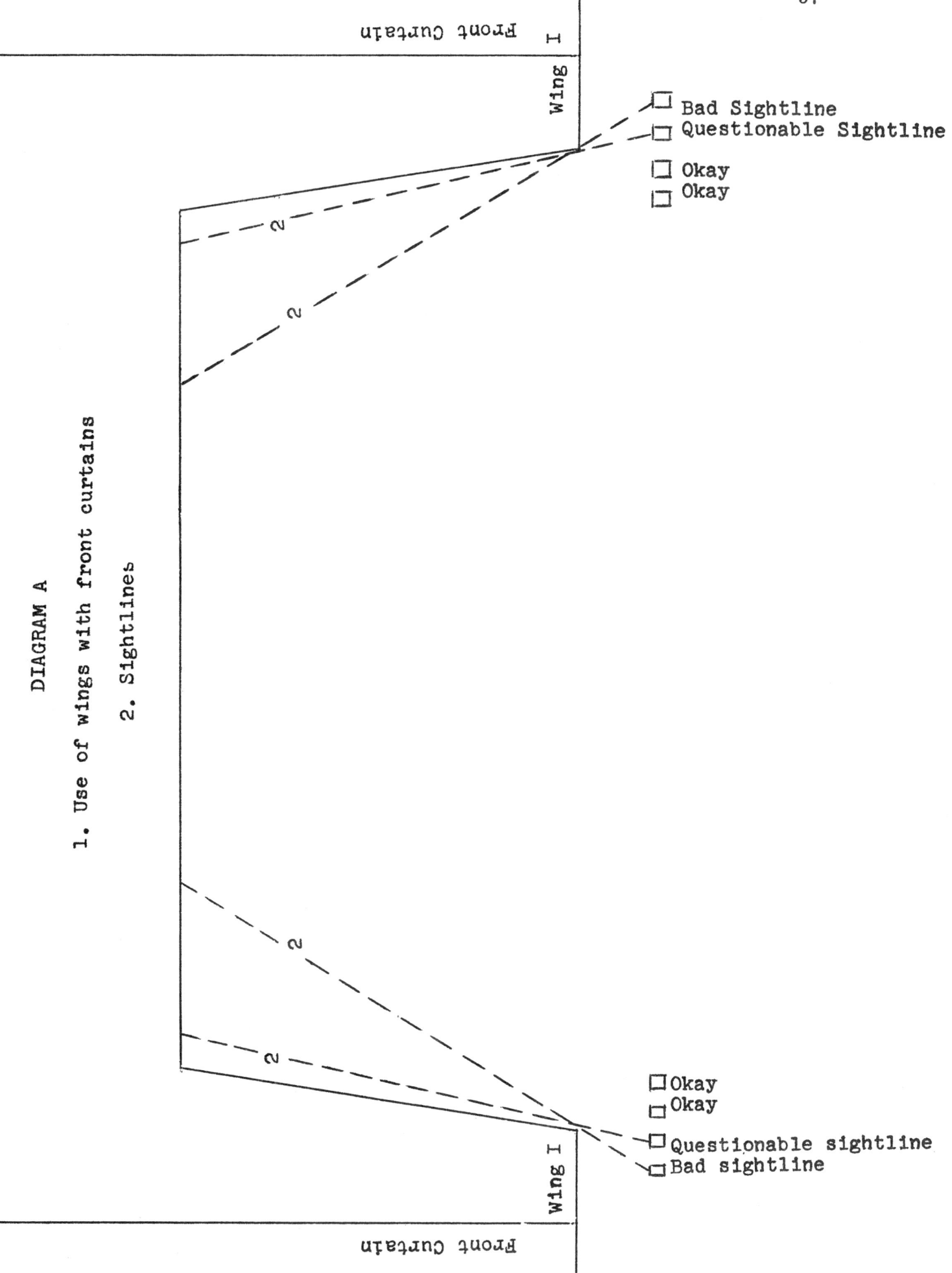

from the original is your major task before you have the first reading rehearsal. It can be done satisfactorily, however. I do not believe a play should be selected only to fit a set; rather, your available set should be made to fit the play. Were you to follow the first course, you would in a short time run out of available plays and, I am afraid, of enthusiastic audiences.

On the other hand, there are a large number of plays, both modern and period, which can be done without any scenery at all, except possibly an opaque backdrop. All of Shakespeare's plays fall in this category. Of the modern plays the following require virtually no scenery: <u>The Robe</u>, <u>The Remarkable Incident at Carson Corners</u>, <u>Rebel Without a Cause</u>, <u>Luther</u>, <u>Tom Jones</u>, and even the popular <u>The Mouse That Roared</u>. There are others, too, although marked for sets, that can be done before curtains. With this kind of play, blocking becomes a worthwhile challenge. There are five steps, I believe, necessary for success with curtain plays:

1. Use steps and platforms with special lighting areas effects.
2. Use a number of hanging spotlights on dimmers for all necessary lighting of the stage.
3. You need a stage and a theatre that can be completely blacked out with the exception of the exit lights.
4. Interiors are merely suggested by the use of a few pieces of furniture; and exteriors are suggested by a bench or plant.
5. Costumes will help with the illusion.

The use of platforms or steps, or both, offers many possibilities for creating acting areas and getting special effects. Secondly, by blacking out your stage with the use of spotlights or dimmers, one can have a fast-moving show going from scene to scene without delays to shift scenery. Musicals can easily be produced with curtains. Scrim curtains become even more effective.

But I repeat: The success of plays with curtains depends on spotlights and blackouts. Timing must be excellent throughout the whole play. A too slow or too fast light may catch characters moving on or off stage--may even catch your overalled property man changing scenery. But this kind of play is a delight to block, to rehearse, and to present.

But let us get back to your homework--blocking the play. First of all, let me state that I firmly believe that "angle" blocking is the most satisfactory. All areas of the stage are important, not just up center stage. The whole stage is the "acting area" and must be so used. Exits and entrances must be well rehearsed. The use of hand properties requires detailed study and effective rehearsal. Any movement on stage must have a motive behind it.

ANGLE BLOCKING

Whether you have only one or two, or twenty characters on stage, your most pleasing pictures will be the "angle" method. With a single character on stage, the furniture creates the angle (Diagram B). Let this single character move down center, and there goes your picture. Your furniture properties lose their effectiveness immediately. When soliloquies are presented from any downstage position, your audience will feel that such actors are speaking directly to them as an orator or debater. Such is not the case, for the audience is not a part of the show. An audience is a "peeping Tom," watching through the "Fourth Wall." Granted, there are a number of shows in which the audience plays its part, as in The Night of January 16th and in the melodramas of another day with their many "asides"; but most of our dramas today are written as if there were no audience--who, by the way, came to see, not to participate in the play. The other drawings will illustrate further this "angle" blocking.

USING ALL AREAS OF STAGE

In observing a number of high school plays I have noticed that one sign of poor blocking is the stage centering of characters. This can result from following the author's directions or the lack of them or the director's belief that center stage is the only important position. When this is happening, chairs to the far right and left are never used. Thus movement becomes static and when there are large casts the playing area becomes crowded. Often as I observed this poor blocking I felt like shouting, "spread out" and "get out of each other's way." No stage setting must be so large that the actors cannot move easily and quickly to all areas. No author intended it to be otherwise.

On the other hand, intimacy can be destroyed by distance. With just two characters on stage, for example, it is unrealistic to have them converse intimately and intelligently with one sitting at the far right and the other standing far left. Why would two people shout across a room while conversing with each other? Blocking is merely a question of awareness--awareness of positions people take in real life.

EXITS AND ENTRANCES

Why do directors assume that

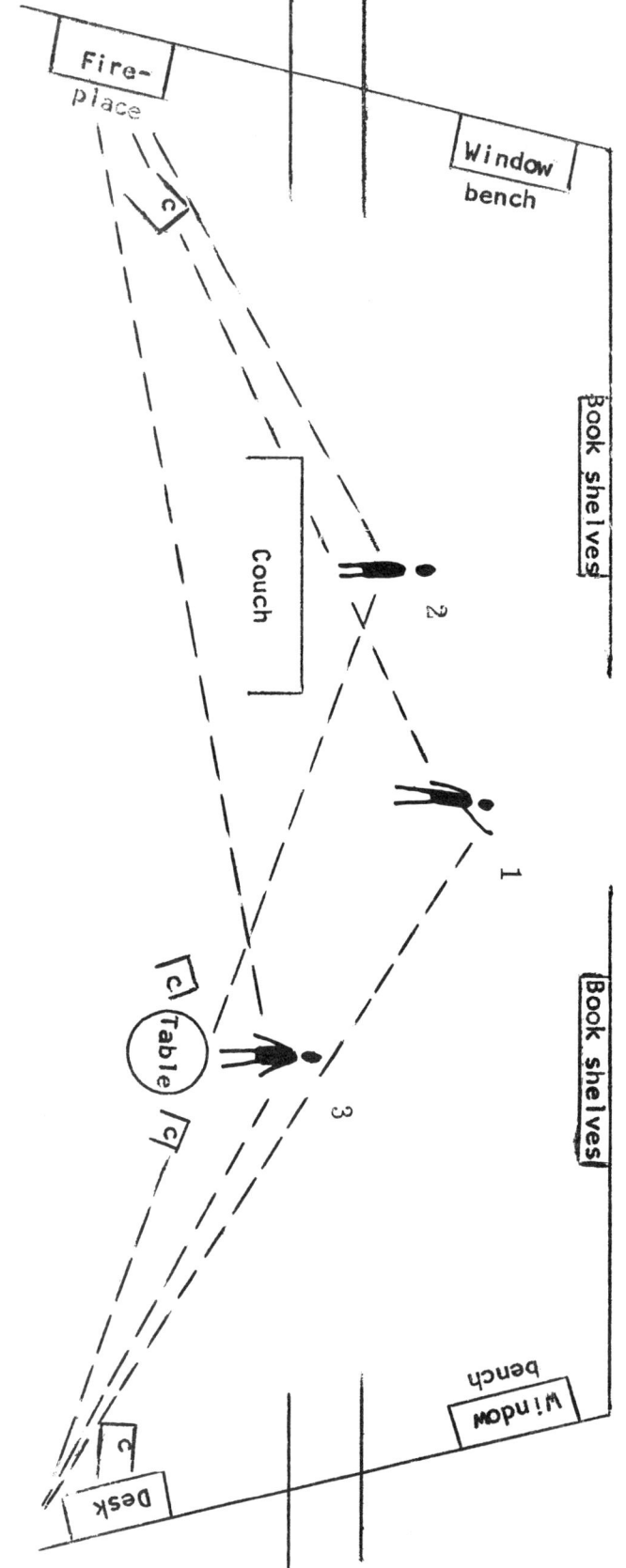

1. In center stage
2. Behind couch
3. Behind table

DIAGRAM B

(One character - angle blocking)

DIAGRAM C

(Several characters - angle blocking)

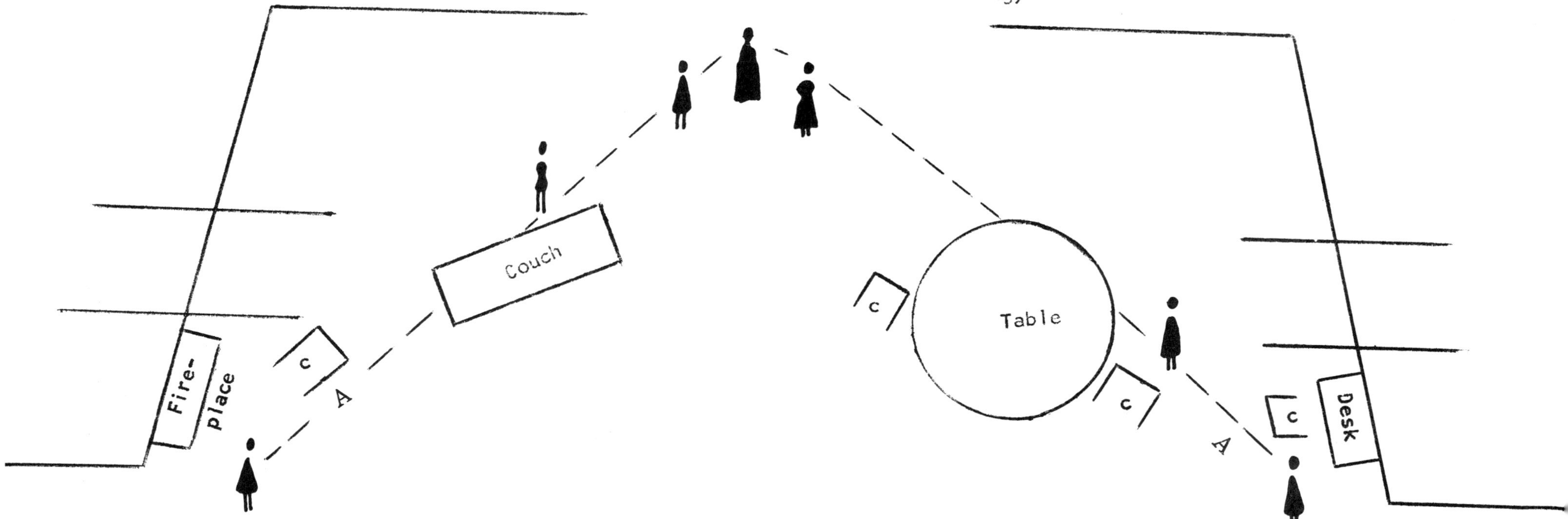

A. Center stage
B. Right center stage 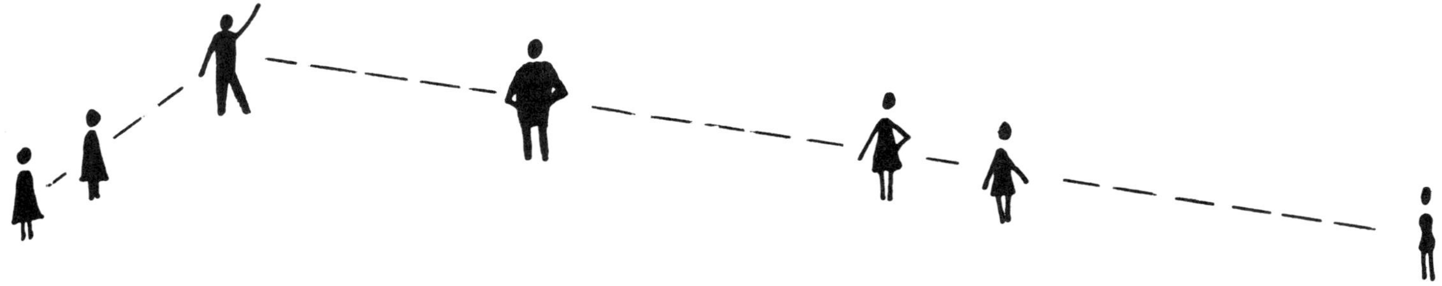
C. Character can be moved to any number of positions

41

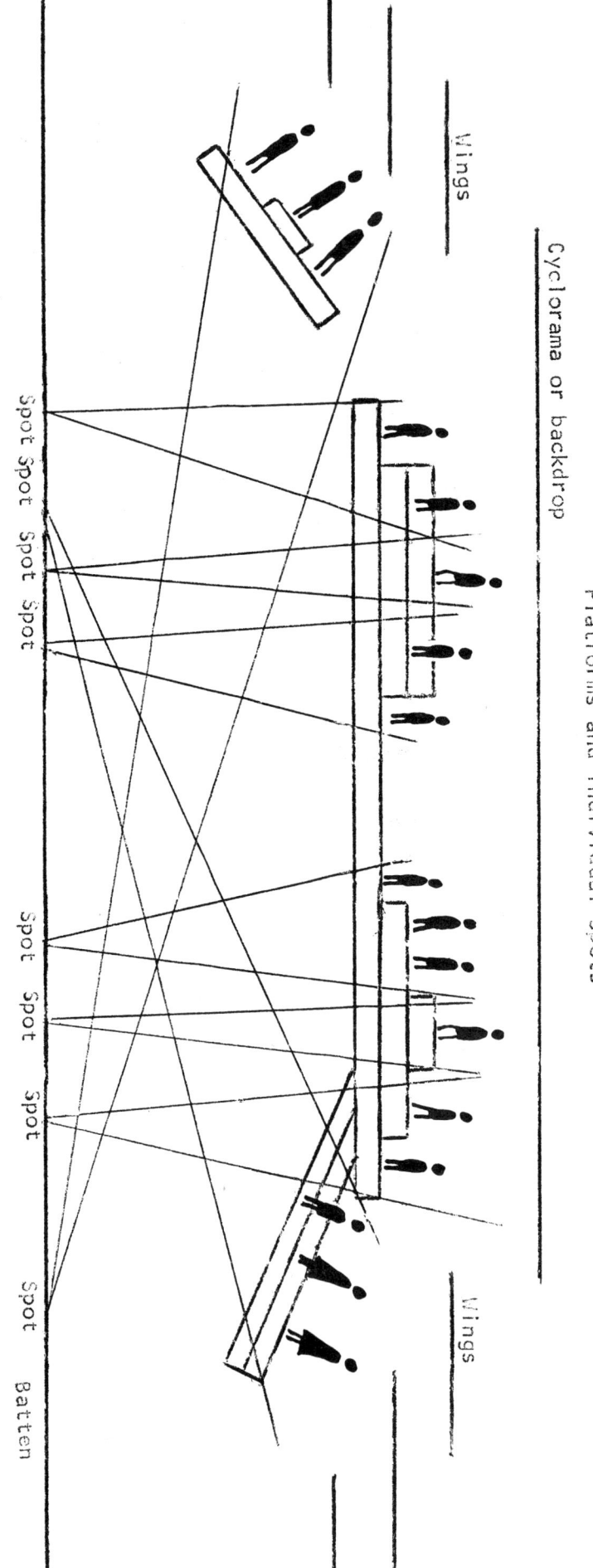

DIAGRAM D

exits and entrances need not be rehearsed? Probably they feel that their young actors know how to open and close doors, exit through a center opening into a hallway, walk upstairs, or even crawl out of windows without directions. Maybe they think coming on and off stage is not important. How wrong they are!

Let's take entrances first. The first step to take for a good entrance is to convince your audience that you are coming from somewhere--the supermarket, office, or school. Thus one assumes the role backstage before he ever opens any door. He must be coming from the supermarket, the office, or school, and the audience recognizes this immediately. Secondly, one's entrance is affected by weather: certainly coming in the room when it is raining or snowing outside will be different from an entrance on a nice day; and an entrance when it is zero weather will be different from that of a very hot day. Next, his entrance will show different emotions--as they are called for whether it is anger, happiness, anxiety, or serenity. You cannot create these emotions as you open the door, they must be a part of you backstage before you put your hand on the doorknob.

Another common fault is entering with your back to the audience. (Yes, this still happens.) If the script calls for this kind of entrance, so be it. But rarely will you find such entrances called for. Whether the doors open upstage toward the back stage wall or upstage on the stage, the entrance should be the same. If the door is in the left side wall, open the door with your right hand, take a step or two on stage, then turn facing the audience and close the door with your left hand. The reverse is true when the door is on the right stage wall. In other words, face the audience; do not turn your back to them. If you have packages or suitcases, place them wherever they are to go and then go back and shut the door. A casual character might kick a door shut if his hands are full of packages.

Exits follow the same procedure. Open the door in the left stage wall with your left hand, step out and turn and close it with your right hand. Of course, if you have a package under one arm, then make a natural exit. Yet by carrying the package in your right hand, you can still exit partially facing the audience. Better still, rehearse so that some one else opens and closes the door for you.

For entrances from a center hallway there usually are no problems; nor are there any on coming downstairs. Exits, however, can be poorly made. For the center exit, one should move on lines toward the archway and then deliver his exit line in or close to the archway. On stairs, deliver your last line after climbing one or two steps. The rule is: <u>Face the audience.</u>

Finally, the last point I wish to stress is that the actor should be near his exit on his last line so that he can get off the stage fast. Nothing is more distracting than to have one deliver his exit line on left stage or even center stage and then watch him walk across the stage to a door in the right wall. Good blocking will have all characters move on their lines toward their exits. As you came from somewhere on your entrance, you are going somewhere on your exit. <u>And stay in character until that door is closed.</u>

HAND PROPERTIES

As soon as books are out of your actors' hands, then make sure they start using hand properties. Do not wait until dress rehearsal week. Whether or not you have the actual hand properties is unimportant, just so the actors pick up and lay down something on cue. More about this later. Now let's consider only the table telephone and lights on tables or stands.

Probably the most devastating property is the telephone. How does one pick it up to call someone or to answer a call? For illustrative purposes assume the telephone is on the right top of the desk shown in the diagrams. Pick up the telephone only with the left hand, never the right hand; then face left just far enough so that the telephone will not cover your face as you talk into it. Likewise, by using your left hand you avoid having the telephone cord running across your body. Unimportant, you say? What's attractive about a character with a telephone cord wrapped around him and a telephone covering his face? Secondly, there is now no danger of pulling the telephone box off the desk.

As far as lamps are concerned, it is important during rehearsals to go through the action of turning them on and off, if the action calls for it, even though the lamps will not be available until the dress rehearsals. This is the only way you can be sure the lamps will be turned on or off at the actual performances. Your young actors can easily forget this action unless it has been rehearsed again and again.

MOVEMENTS ON STAGE

The directions state "moves to sofa and sits down"; "walks to fireplace"; "to behind table." So we follow directions and come up with a stilted play. Are we thus to ignore directions? Absolutely not. The author had a reason for inserting these directions. Your job is to find out why.

One simply does not move about the stage, sit in a chair, rise from a chair, or pick up a property unless he is so motivated. There is something in the lines or some action on stage that calls for moving from one spot to another, for sitting, for rising--and it is up to you to find these cues. Shakespeare's plays give no directions; the lines tell one what he must do. Of course the ringing of the telephone will take one to the desk. A line that reads, "Am I tired tonight!" will suggest the easy chair or the sofa. Anxiety about someone who is not home yet will take one frequently to the windows or to the outside door. Anger can easily call for one to rise from a chair and pace the floor. The point here is that there must be a reason for any movement--one that your audience can justifiably accept.

Once this homework is done, you should have all the answers about the blocking of the play. You are done with the scenery set board, the doll furniture, and the checkers and chessmen. You are now ready to move live people about the stage. The rehearsals are now "on the road." But do not throw your blocking material too far away, for you may have to come back to it tomorrow night!

Chapter Five

TECHNICAL ORGANIZATION

Too often, I am afraid, too much emphasis is placed on the actors on stage. But their success could not have been achieved without the aid of the backstage, the promotion, and the "front-of-the-house" crews. The director is of course proud of his cast when they receive deserved congratulations. But he knows that those who stand in the shadows contributed a major part in winning those curtain calls and congratulations. Interpretation and characterization belong to the actor, but a great deal of what the audience sees was achieved by those who worked so hard for several weeks behind the scenes.

The responsibility for each performance rests solely with the director, regardless of how many faculty or student assistants he may have selected. The director will find that he must plan to meet with all his personnel at different times during the six weeks' preparation. He will have to check progress being made in all areas. He will also have, at times, the difficult problem of settling arguments and relieving tensions. You don't make assignments in theatre production and then assume that at the first dress rehearsal all assignments will be satisfactorily completed.

My own experience and those of others have convinced me that you need four assistant directors: technical, onstage, promotional, and financial. In well-organized school drama departments these directors are members of the faculty who receive additional compensation for the required overtime. For example, in one school system the school board annually budgeted $600 for such compensation. Then the board left the selection of the faculty directors and the amount to be paid to the director. However, in most schools throughout the country such ideal situations do not exist. The only help available is that of student directors and student committee chairmen--which requires checking and double checking to make sure they are completing the assigned tasks.

TECHNICAL DIRECTOR

The duties of the Technical Director are essentially to supervise stage crews. These are usually broken down into scenery, properties, and lighting crews. Naturally he will appoint chairmen of these three crews who will be responsible solely to him. He will need to buy materials to build scenery, such as paints, glue, and sizing for the painting of scenery. He must be, in addition, a teacher--one who can pass this information on to his crews.

Secondly, it is also his responsibility to assemble all movable stage properties, such as tables, desks, chairs, and lamps. He must be acquainted so well with the play that he knows the period of the play and what kind of furniture is required. It is important to watch the size of the furniture in order to have a well-balanced stage. Too often stages are cluttered with too many furniture pieces that are too large. Be sure that there is enough space so your cast can move about with ease. On the other hand, there can also be too little furniture on a large stage.

Third, lighting the set is his last, but very important, assignment. Spots must be wired, hung, and focused; the necessary colors need to be put into the spots and tested. Footlights and border lights, if they are used, need to be checked. The dimmer board has to be hooked up and then tested. Finally, a light cue sheet must be completed and run through before dress rehearsals.

I have mentioned only briefly the duties and responsibilities of backstage crews. No attempt will be included here on how to build scenery, paint it, or what kinds of period furniture to use. Nor will I deal with what kind of spotlights to buy, or how to rig them. There are excellent texts on these subjects now available, of which I recommend How to Produce the Play by John Wray Young and Margaret Mary Young, now in its fourth printing and published by the Dramatic Publishing Company.

On the other hand, both the director and the technical director must be well trained in building and painting scenery. They should know about period furniture and stage lighting. This leads me to my final thought. The decision of the set design and the color of the paint to be used is that of the director--not that of the technical director. One must never lose sight of the fact that the success or failure of a performance rests solely on the director's shoulders. A good technical director will know what kind of scenery the play calls for, how it is to be lighted, and what furniture is required--and he will make his suggestions known to the director, who will then make all final decisions. There must be no public disagreement between these two at any time during the preparation of the performances.

ON-STAGE DIRECTOR

The duties of the On-stage Director are the assembling of hand props, the selection of costumes, and the application of the correct make-up. Too often one assumes that the hand props are the responsibility of the members of the cast who will use them. Granted, the actor must double-check all hand props on the nights of the performances; but it is not his responsibility to see that the gloves are on the table, that the revolver is in the drawer of the desk, or that the letter is between the covers of a magazine. The on-stage director and his props committee have a check list of all hand props, and the items are not only placed on stage where they belong, but also checked backstage to see that they are on the hand props table so they are available for the actor on his entrance. Likewise, all hand props are collected at the close of each scene and replaced on the prop table. One missing hand prop can ruin your whole show.

Costuming any play is a real problem. Unfortunately one may assume that costuming pertains only to period plays. Nothing could be further from the truth. For example, let's take a modern play which requires several changes of clothing. First of all, the on-stage director must know the colors of the set and the colors of the furniture. With this knowledge he then meets with the cast and informs them of the color of clothes which will be acceptable. All dresses and suits must be brought to school before dress rehearsals in order to check style and color. Do not ever have a female character sit down on a sofa with a dress that conflicts with the colors of the slip cover. Do not have your two leads dressed so that the colors of his sport jacket are in direct contrast with the colors of her dress. There must be harmony in color--scenery with costumes; costumes with furniture; costumes with costumes.

For period plays, one recognizes immediately these same problems mentioned above. Of course the best policy for period plays is to rent the costumes. Too expensive, you say? Probably so, but do you realize that a part of the rental charge is the professional help you are receiving?

Of the many plays I did during my twenty years as a high school director--straight plays, both modern and period; pageants; musicals-- I, as director, went directly to the costumer and with his help selected my costumes, thus being sure of the proper color harmonies. If a special kind of costume was required, as in a specialty number of a musical, I had the costumer make the costume for me, for which I paid a slightly higher rental. I also found that I needed the advice of the costumer concerning wigs, both male and female, and concerning period hand props, such as canes, swords, and handkerchiefs. To me the cost of the rentals was really cheap considering the time saved in research. Secondly, I always felt secure, too, for the costumes with wigs and hand props were exactly right for the period of the play. Children's costumes usually have to be made, as, for example, for the children in The King and I.

With the arrival of the costumes, usually a week to ten days before the performance, the on-stage director calls together all members of the cast to try on all costumes. In most cases only minor adjustments have to be made. Hand properties should then be made available for the next rehearsal.

If you make your own costumes (excellent training, I am afraid, only for the mothers of the cast), your problems are selection of pattern, selection of materials (silk, velvet, wool, or cotton), and selection of complimentary colors of materials. You may still have to rent wigs and certain hand props from a costumer. The on-stage director must check all samples of material before it is purchased so that he is sure the colors will not conflict with the scenery, furniture, and other costumes. Finally, as soon as the costumes are finished, they should be brought to school for the final approval of the director.

As one of his last responsibilities, the on-stage director is in charge of the make-up crew. One is aware that in the commercial theatre the actors do their own make-up. In some high schools members of the cast do likewise. However, in most high schools, make-up crews are students trained, I hope, in stage make-up. Again I am ignoring the technicalities. Since there are many available texts on this subject, I offer only the following suggestions:

1. Any make-up that is discernible beyond the first five rows of the auditorium is too heavy. Do not make up for the people in the last row of the auditorium for no matter how heavy you make the make-up, they won't be able to see it anyway.
2. All visible parts of the body must be made up. This means face, ears, neck, and hands. One's face cannot be that of an old woman, while her hands and arms are those of the high school student.
3. Merely placing a mustache or beard on a young face is not enough to portray age. Eyes and foreheads, too, must

suggest the age of the character. The appearance of youth must be completely deleted.
4. Merely drawing lines on one's forehead or cheeks or chin will not suggest age. Age lines should never be visible.
5. Make-up should be applied at all dress rehearsals so it can be checked by both the director and the on-stage director while the character is on stage. Often your stage lighting will require some adjustment.
6. Cast members, made up and costumed, should not be permitted to go to the front of the theatre at any time, nor should incoming audience members be permitted in the areas set aside backstage for cast and crews. Why reveal part of your show before the curtain opens?
7. Finally, all make-up must be completely removed before the cast is permitted to leave the building. Each cast member should report to the on-stage director for checking-out privileges.

PROMOTIONAL DIRECTOR

After from four to six weeks of extensive rehearsals, director, cast, and crews expect sizable and appreciative audiences to see their play. With just a handful of people seated in a large auditorium, the cast will lose heart before the curtain is ever opened. Thus the work of the Promotional Director during the six weeks of rehearsals is all-important in assuring the success of the play--or better still, the success of the entire theatre program of the school. The enthusiasm and the amount of energy expended by the promotional committee is another real contribution.

The first major project is the creation of attractive posters. One of the methods used successfully in a number of schools is a poster contest. Posters are judged and awards given. However, all posters should be put on display, not only in school but in store windows throughout the community. When pictures of members of the cast are available, they should be used on the posters.

Other publicity stunts that have proven helpful in Thespian-affiliated schools are as follows:
1. Printing the title of the play on cafeteria napkins.
2. Daily and weekly announcements over school public address system.
3. Introducing the cast and presenting several interesting cuttings from the play at a general assembly.
4. Talented speakers made available for Service Club luncheons.

One certainly can add to the above list with just a little more imagination. However, publicity stunts must always be in good taste and have approval from the school administration.

If the school has a weekly newspaper, your promotion news editor should prepare interesting news items about incidents at rehearsals. These can involve items about the play itself, such as its Broadway run, its popularity with other schools (best illustrated in the annual Thespian survey). There can be photographs of cast and crews at work preparing the production. For the daily city newspapers, articles should be submitted infrequently for the first four weeks of the rehearsals, and then one or two well worthwhile articles the week before the actual presentation. One good announcement over the local radio or TV station is the best one can hope for--and it has to be unusual to obtain even a little public service spot. A paid advertisement in city papers may be effective, but not on radio or TV--they are much too expensive. Warning: be sure no part of the play itself is publicly printed or read or acted on radio or TV without special permission of the publisher. Violation of the copyright laws can be very expensive.

The printed program also is another duty of the promotional director, if the program carries paid advertisements. In soliciting advertising, a real promotional job must be done. Your salesman must make the potential customer feel that his advertisement will pay dividends in increasing sales. His advertisement is not to be considered as a public service, or, even worse, a gift. All advertisers should receive two complimentary tickets.

If the program does not include advertisements, then the program committee can easily be under the direction of the on-stage director. To whomever this job is assigned, one must be sure that he knows how to edit, lay out pages, proofread correctly, and estimate the actual number needed. A poorly prepared program, carelessly printed, loaded with misspellings and poorly laid out, will immediately create wrong impressions. The program must be something worth taking home, not something to leave behind on the floor of the auditorium.

FINANCIAL DIRECTOR

One responsibility that is often overlooked is that of the Financial Director. His duties are what I like to call "front-of-house" duties. He is directly responsible for the printing of all tickets, presales of tickets, box office sales, and the training of the ushers. Probably his position demands more tact than any other, for he comes in contact with the public most frequently. He must be polite, understanding, and quietly efficient. He cannot afford to become confused or frustrated, for he is handling the actual money. He must be sure all money collected from students for advance ticket sales is correct, that exchange of tickets--yes, even refunds--are cheerfully handled. Finally he must at times dolefully, not cheerfully, inform potential customers that the show is completely sold out, and extend to them an invitation to attend the next performance. Finally, he must prepare an accurate financial account of the completed ticket sales within one week following the last performance.

As your audience assembles, your ushers take on importance in your over-all theatre program. We sometimes take ushering too lightly, thus creating bad impressions before the curtain is ever opened. To me the usher is a host or hostess. He must be properly and neatly dressed, for he is the first to greet your arriving guests. Male ushers in Tuxedos or dark blue suits make an attractive appearance; female ushers in formal dress are always impressive. If the play is a period piece, why not rent additional costumes of the period for the ushers? It will make them feel as if they are truly a part of the play, and it will create an atmosphere of the period before the show begins.

As you read on through this chapter you may have felt that you have traveled farther and farther away from the director, that he has a "soft" job because he has so many other persons doing assigned tasks, that his sole responsibility is directing the play through the rehearsal weeks, and that all the pieces will fall in place at the first dress rehearsal. No director will ever be so lucky, especially in the high school theatre!

The director double-checks all along the line--scenery, costumes, lighting, program, advance ticket sales, posters, ushers--for he is the one, the only one, who makes the final decisions. It is his play from the selection through the final performance. And good directors will have it no other way.

Chapter Six

PROJECTION

The set is beautiful, the costuming superb, the blocking could not be better, the interpretations and characterizations are excellent-- and yet the audience is "cold." They are not laughing at the funny lines, nor are they reacting to the emotional scenes with the sounds so recognizable by experienced actors. They even seem restless and to some extent noisy. What is wrong? The answer is simple: They cannot <u>hear</u> the play. To them it has become a silent movie, a pantomime --and in this day and age of TV, sound systems, public address systems, and radio, silence is a novelty with which they have lost contact. One does not have to <u>listen</u> today, for all one has to do is to turn a knob to increase the volume of sound.

In my judgment "live" theatre, both commercial and non-commercial, faces its biggest challenge in the projection of the human voice from the stage to the last rows of the theatre. The art of listening has been reduced to mere conversational pieces at home, in the office, and around the luncheon table. All other sound is projected for us by superb sound and speaker systems--at the movies, at night clubs, at the commercial theatre and musicals, at banquets, and at most national conventions. We no longer are forced to listen with our own ears; rather, we now listen mechanically as part of a mass audience.

The human voice likewise loses its tone qualities due to sound systems--sometimes for the better, often for the worse. Certain vocalists would be total failures without their microphones; others, failures with them. Certain public speakers could not be heard beyond the first five rows of the auditorium without sound systems; others refuse to use systems of any kind.

The medium hurt most of all by lack of sound is the straight play. For some reason or other, use of speaker systems for plays has not been too satisfactory. Some success has been achieved by hanging several microphones overhead, but just out of sight of the audience. On other occasions a string of microphones is run across the front of the stage at the footlights. Unfortunately, these attempts have not been too successful due to the fact that there are spaces on stage which microphones will not reach. This produces contrasting loud and soft voices. Due to the mechanical qualities of all voices, one loses tone inflection; inadequate amplifiers throughout the auditorium can produce deaf spots. An adequate sound system, especially for the high school theatre, can be very expensive.

What does all this add up to? Only one thing: The drama teacher must also be a speech teacher. Certainly he can ease his problem somewhat by paying particular attention to enunciation and pronunciation, to tone qualities, and to the richness of the voices at try-outs. Unfortunately, he is looking for actors and actresses, not orators or public speakers. Thus, even in casting, he may be forced to select students who unwillingly and perhaps unknowingly have bad speech habits.

Early in the rehearsals every effort must be made to break these habits. The use of tape recorders is highly recommended so that students can hear themselves speak and thus become aware of their slovenly speech. Secondly, your cast must be made aware that they are not conversing with each other on stage, but rather with that person in the last row of the theatre. They must be taught that the consonants of our alphabet are just as important as the vowels. The _d's_ and _t's_ and the _ing's_ must be pronounced clearly. They must learn that their voices are like megaphones, that they must open their mouths wide to let the sound out, that they must direct the breath stream toward their front teeth, that certain words in each speech, usually the nouns and verbs, must be stressed and that the first word of his speech is slightly emphasized in picking up cues, and that the last words of any one speech must not be "dropped."

Finally, as the rehearsals improve in quality, which can mean that the lines are solidly memorized and the blocking is completed, then certain students and faculty members should be asked to sit in at rehearsals. They should be placed in different areas of the auditorium with only one objective in mind, to see whether they not only hear the lines but can understand them. Other members of the cast, as well as the director, are not eligible to be listening posts, for in most cases they too unconsciously have memorized the lines from the constant repetition of them at rehearsals. They feel sure they "hear and understand" each word, but actually they are only repeating their own memorizations. If your listening posts can hear the speeches in an empty auditorium with its poor acoustics and resounding noises, then you can be fairly sure that your play will be heard at the opening performance.

Of all the straight plays I have seen over the years my one outstanding criticism is the lack of projection by the cast. This is true both in the commercial and the non-commercial theatres. No matter how excellent and beautiful are the scenery, costumes, and the lighting, the whole play is lost if your audience cannot hear what is being said on stage. I am afraid that in too many productions projection by the cast is taken for granted, whereas it should be the most rehearsed element during the weeks of rehearsals. A blind person can enjoy all that he can hear, for the spoken word alone can create pictures of untold beauty. But without the words, a picture remains just a picture.

Chapter Seven

DRESS REHEARSALS

By the time casts, crews and directors reach the dress rehearsal week, all plans have been completed, all work done, and all cue sheets studied and understood. Whatever delays there may occur now are caused by some minor detail overlooked in the original planning. The director whose philosophy is that bad dress rehearsals foresee successful performances is only kidding himself--not his crews nor his cast. Dress rehearsals should build confidence, not destroy self-assurance.

The number of dress rehearsals will be determined by the play itself. The minimum should be two--and the maximum, five. The latter is especially true for lengthy musical comedies with the many changes of scenery and costumes, the complicated lighting, its large casts of soloists, choruses, and dancers; and with its attendant problems of musical scores. Costume plays may need three dress rehearsals so that the cast can learn to walk, to sit and rise from chairs and benches gracefully without embarrassment. They also need to acquaint themselves further with hand props.

Likewise, make-up must be checked against the lighting--and it takes two rehearsals to do just that satisfactorily. To me a dress rehearsal is merely a checking and double-checking process--timing, voices, and movement. Dress rehearsals should never be a continuation of rehearsals, but rather the epitome of all rehearsals, superseded only by the performances themselves.

Here the director takes full charge by issuing orders, by stopping the running of the show whenever slips occur either with cast, scenery, or lighting, and by consulting his <u>invited listening posts</u> concerning projection. Here he is the stern, unforgiving taskmaster when slips occur. He tolerates no foolishness on stage, backstage, or in the auditorium. He is now the strict disciplinarian, for he is aware that the degree of discipline separating success from failure is indeed very small. One bad break may lose a football game; one visible misjudgment may ruin a play. No detail is so little that it can be ignored.

It may be necessary to hold separate scenery and light rehearsals, especially for musicals. When sets have to be changed during the action of the play, not between scenes and acts, such rehearsals are necessary in order to achieve exact timing. I recall one of my original musicals in which the curtain opened on a college dormitory room scene. This was at the opening of the song, then the curtain closed as the soloist walked downstage. The scene was completely changed behind the curtain during the song, to an exterior scene with a backdrop, benches, and suggested trees for a dance number that followed. Then, after the dance we went back to the soloist as the scene reverted to the dormitory scene and ended as the soloist sat down on the last note of the song. At the first scene rehearsal the stage crew said it could not be done in the time allotted. They couldn't remove furniture, drop the exterior back curtain into place, set the benches and trees, then later remove the benches and trees, raise the exterior curtain and bring back the dormitory furniture. But after several rehearsals, and after definite assignments were made to each crew member, it was done easily. The scene was one of the outstanding numbers of the show. With pageants, the above timing problem has to be even more carefully scheduled, for usually there is a speaker on stage who keeps the scenes moving without interruption.

Scenery has to be changed and the cast assembled on and off stage in even shorter time than is usually required for musicals.

Lighting cues and sound effects also require special attention. One rehearsal with soloists and dance numbers may be necessary when booth spots are used. The cast members involved should be present at the light rehearsals. Finally, all members of the cast should at least walk on stage under any special lighting to check the effects of that lighting, especially if colors are used, on their costumes.

Special costume rehearsals may be needed. In The Barretts of Wimpole Street the director may wish to ape the Broadway production by having the female characters walk without moving the large hoop skirts of that period. If so, this requires practice backstage and a special rehearsal. Also, your female cast members must learn how to sit and rise with their costumes on. If this practice is not included in the schedule, the girls may be embarrassed on sitting down when their hoops rise nearly above their heads. They must be taught that in some special costumes they only sit on the front of the chairs. In children's plays, special costume rehearsals may be necessary for those playing animal parts. A costume change while the show is in progress may have to be practiced so that the character returns to the show on cue.

Soloists and dance numbers should be rehearsed with the orchestra both for cues and timing. Usually these rehearsals can be arranged before dress rehearsal at the call of the orchestra director. In other words, when the orchestra has really learned the musical score of the show, then he should request soloists, choruses, and dancers to rehearse with him at one of his regularly scheduled rehearsals.

With all these preparations made before or early in the week of dress rehearsal, the final two rehearsals should run smoothly and satisfactorily for all concerned. Basically it all boils down to intensive rehearsals and strict attention to all of the details during the entire time the show is in preparation.

At the final two dress rehearsals the director's chief concern should be the following:

1. Timing

    Is the show moving, not dragging in any one spot? Are all cues --lines, lights, scenery, orchestra--being picked up rapidly and on time?

2. Blocking

    The director should move around the auditorium--along both sides and down front particularly --to see that the sight lines are good. Make sure the people sitting on the end side seats can see all the action on stage at all times. They deserve this consideration, for they probably paid as much for their tickets as did those in the center section.

3. Projection

    Again faculty guests, seated in certain sections of the auditorium, including the balcony, should be checked repeatedly throughout the performance to find out whether or not they can hear the spoken lines. If not, rather than stop the show, notes should be made for a later discussion with the guilty cast members.

4. Scenery and lighting

    This is the time for a final checking on effectiveness. The question to keep in mind here is: Are you creating the effect you want? Again your guests can help you answer this question. One must never forget, insofar as lighting is concerned, not to get so carried away with special effects that your audience can't see the action.

5. Costumes

    Has your cast learned its lesson well concerning the wearing of costumes and the use of hand props, especially if this involves guns and swords? If not, take notes for further discussion and rehearsal.

6. Make-up

Is your committee practicing what you "preached"? Not too heavy, characters well pictured, beards looking natural, all visible parts of the body made up --hands, legs, ears, and neck? What does the lighting do to the make-up?

Finally, dress rehearsals should not be interrupted for further direction. It is now time to let the show take its course. What little direction there is, offered at the last rehearsals, is inconsequential. Really it is too late now to make any further minor changes. To me the final dress rehearsal is the opening performance. Anything less than that shows poor planning somewhere along the line.

Chapter Eight

THE PERFORMANCE

On the night of the first performance and for the following presentations, if the show runs two or more nights, the director still has responsibilities. Actually his responsibilities do not end until the final curtain at the last performance. For the director who walks out on his cast and crews on opening night with the admonition that they are now running the show is, in my judgment, deserting from an important school project. The director belongs backstage during the entire performance--not out front sitting with the audience. He still must check and double-check constantly while the show is on. Snap decisions may have to be made because of some unforeseen incident; as, a back-drop caught on ropes, fuse burned out in one of the electric plates, illness of a cast or crew member due to the excitement, a hand property missing--so many things can happen throughout a performance. It is the director's job to render immediate decisions to cover up all of these unexpected problems. It is still his show whether he wants to so acknowledge it or not.

In outline form the directorial duties on opening night are as follows:

1. Check to see both cast and crews arrive at the set time.

2. Intermittently check the costumes and make-up until nearly curtain time.

3. Check stage to see that the set is solidly in place for the opening scene.

4. Open the curtain on the set with all stage lights on and before the audience is let in. Then go sit in the auditorium and stare at the set for some time--thus you can check that every piece of furniture is in its right place.

5. Require the cast, one by one, to come on stage for one last check on their make-up.

6. Visit the box-office and the corridor to the auditorium to see that both your financial director and ushers are prepared for the opening of the doors.

7. Be sure programs are available--you don't want them left in your office or in the principal's office.

8. Make a final check of the auditorium--are the curtains closed, the orchestra lights in place, the

dim foots or spots on the curtain in order to create the right theatrical atmosphere?

9. Then a final signal should come, from director only, to open the front doors.

10. Check your cast to see that they are in the assigned room after they are dressed and made up. Do not permit the cast on stage at any time prior to curtain time.

11. There should be a final warning to crews on stage that there is no peeping through the curtain at the audience. Don't let anyone from backstage into the auditorium after the front doors open.

12. Have a final meeting with the cast for a few quick words of encouragement--not for any further instructions or admonitions. Rather, let them feel that you are sure that this is a good show, superbly cast, and well dressed; that you know they will do a superb job, for they are well trained; and finally, tell them that it is now their show. Be brief with your encouraging remarks and don't make it a "pep" talk.

13. On signal, the entire cast takes its place on stage. Do not make those characters who may appear only in the second or third acts remain alone in some room. Let them get the feel of the show as it develops.

14. Between scenes and acts, leave the cast and crew alone. If they are well trained, they will be too busy and too excited and concerned to be bothered further by the director.

15. Between acts, if the director is so inclined, he can go "out front" to hear comments from the audience, especially as to whether or not they can hear the spoken lines. At this time a director should not be too concerned about likes and dislikes. His attitude must be that you cannot please everyone.

16. After the final curtain, be sure you congratulate your cast for a job well done. Hold them on stage after last curtain call before you let them meet the audience, which usually herds backstage after each performance.

17. Check with all chairmen to see that all props have been returned, costumes checked in, make-up removed before the cast leaves the theatre.

18. Double-check the switchboard when you're done to be sure all switches are pulled so that you will not have a burned-out dimmer plate for the second performance.

19. Double-check your final arrangements to make sure you return all borrowed properties (if any), that costumes are packed for shipment to the costumer, and that make-up supplies are still ample for the next performance.

20. Finally, be doubly sure that you, as director, have thanked all faculty members who served as chairmen of your committees.

So the opening night has come and gone. Six weeks of rehearsals are now behind you. You have received warm congratulations for another successful performance. You have witnessed the delight of your cast at the close of the show, the audience reaction in greeting the members of your cast. Success or failure, who knows but you, the director!

AFTER GLOW

As a director, I found a great deal of satisfaction, at the close of each performance, in remaining alone on stage while the cast and crews were doing their last chores before leaving the theatre. I liked being on stage surrounded by the scenery and furniture, for it gave me a feeling of warmth and satisfaction. Six weeks ago this was a bare stage with dirty walls and a cyclorama; six weeks ago I had selected a group of high school students with little or no theatre experience to mold into a play. Was it worth it--the time, the energy, the forever-lost hours away from my family--for the continued prestige of theatre of this high school?

As I looked about me for a last glance of fantasy, this make-believe, I felt that warmth again that all was well. When I remembered that boy and girl, awkward and shy, such a short time ago, performing so well as a Peter Pan, an Eliza, a Mr. Higgins, an Elizabeth Barrett, or a Robert Browning, I felt sure that I had given to them something that they will cherish for the remainder of their lives.

And then I questioned my choice of play, my direction, my color choices, my lighting, and even my casting, and I wondered whether or not I had erred somewhere, whether or not I could have had an even better play had I done this or that-- which led only to one conclusion: the play, in my own judgment, not that of my friends and associates and students and townspeople, was either successful or a failure. Deep down in my own heart I and only I knew the answer. For here was a thing of love, a dream realized-- not a commercial project whose sole aim was how much money could be made!

Finally, I sensed that through my efforts as director I had offered entertainment for my school and for my community. But most important, this play was an educational experience for these high school students. Here they learned by doing, by working together, meaningful achievements that they can take with them into adult living.

Well, it's all over--the last curtain has fallen, the lights have been dimmed, the scenery has been struck--our next play will be . . . I can hardly wait to get started!

NATIONAL THESPIAN SOCIETY SURVEY

The following are the most frequently produced full-length plays (all categories) by Thespian-affiliated schools starting with the 1960-61 school year through the 1964-65 school year. The list was tabulated from an average of 1800 schools reporting annually over the five-year period. Only those plays with 15 or more productions annually are listed alphabetically, not by the number of productions as submitted yearly.

All Shook Up
Amahl and the Night Visitors
Annie Get Your Gun
Antigone
Arsenic and Old Lace
Ask Any Girl
Blithe Spirit
Brigadoon
Bull in a China Shop
Bye Bye Birdie
Carousel
Charley's Aunt
Cheaper by the Dozen
Cinderella
Connecticut Yankee in King Arthur's Court, A
Courtship of Eddie's Father
Crucible, The
Curious Savage, The
Curtain Going Up
Death and Life of Larry Benson, The
Diary of Anne Frank, The
Denny and the Witches
Dino
Down in the Valley
Family Nobody Wanted, The
Finian's Rainbow
George Washington Slept Here
Glass Menagerie, The

Hansel and Gretel
Harvey
H. M. S. Pinafore
Importance of Being Earnest, The
Inherit the Wind
I Remember Mama
January Thaw
King and I, The
Lil Abner
Little Dog Laughed, The
Little Women
Lock, Stock and Lipstick
Madwoman of Chaillot
Man Who Came to Dinner, The
Many Loves of Dobie Gillis, The
Matchmaker, The
Meet Me in St. Louis
Midsummer Night's Dream, A
Mikado, The
Miracle Worker, The
Mouse That Roared, The
Mousetrap, The
Mrs. McThing
Music Man, The
My Fair Lady
My Three Angels
Night of January 16th, The
Oklahoma
Onions in the Stew

Our Hearts Were Young and Gay
Our Town
Pillow Talk
Pygmalion
Rebel Without a Cause
Rocket in His Pocket
Skin of Our Teeth
Solid Gold Cadillac, The
Sound of Music, The
South Pacific

Stage Door
Swingin' High
Tammy Tell Me True
Teahouse of the August Moon
Ten Little Indians
Time Out for Ginger
Tom Jones
Winnie-the-Pooh
Wizard of Oz, The
Who Dunit?
You Can't Take It With You

NATIONALLY RECOGNIZED PUBLISHERS OF PLAYS AND MUSICALS

Anchorage Press, Cloverlot, Anchorage, Kentucky 40001

Baker's Plays, 100 Summer Street, Boston, Massachusetts 02110

David McKay Company, Inc., 750 Third Avenue, New York, New York 10017

Dramatic Publishing Company, 86 East Randolph Street, Chicago, Illinois 60601

Dramatists Play Service, Inc., 440 Park Avenue South, New York, New York 10016

Eldridge Publishing Company, Franklin, Ohio 45005

Evans Plays, 500 East 77th Street, New York, New York 10021

Music Theatre International, 119 West 57th Street, New York, New York 10019

Plays, Inc., 8 Arlington Street, Boston, Massachusetts 02116

Samuel French, Inc., 25 West 45th Street, New York, New York 10036

Rodger and Hammerstein Repertory, 120 East 56th Street, New York, New York 10022

Tams-Witmark Music Library, Inc., 757 Third Avenue, New York, New York 10017

REFERENCES AND SUGGESTED READING

GALLAWAY, Marian. The Director in the Theatre. The Macmillan Company, New York, 1963.

SIEVERS, W. David. Directing for the Theatre. William C. Brown Company, Dubuque, Iowa, 1965.

THOMAS, Charles. Make-Up. Theatre Arts Books, New York, 1964.

SOUTHERN, Richard. Proscenium and Sight Lines. Theatre Arts Books, New York, 1964.

PAYNE, Blanche. History of Costume from the Ancient Egyptians to the Twentieth Century. Harper and Row, New York, 1965.

MOORE, Sonia. The Stanislavski System. The Viking Press, New York, 1965.

ENTERS, Angna. On Mime. Wesleyan University Press, Middletown, Connecticut, 1965.

PEACHER, Georgiana. How To Improve Your Speaking Voice. Frederick Fell, Inc., New York, 1966.

YOUNG, John Wray and Margaret Mary. How to Produce the Play. Dramatic Publishing Company, Chicago, 1960.

YOUNG, John Wray. Directing the Play. Harper and Brothers, 1958.

WAUGH, Norah. The Cut of Men's Clothes. Theatre Arts Books, New York, 1964.

ADAMS, Harlen Martin. Speak Up. Revised Edition, Macmillan Company, New York, 1964.

FRAAGH and BRINSON, Peggy Van and Peter. The Choreographic Art. Alfred A. Knopf, New York, 1963.

STANISLAVSKI, Constantin. An Actor's Handbook. Theatre Arts Books, New York, 1963.

TOMPKINS, Dorothy Lee. Handbook for Theatrical Apprentices. Samuel French, New York, 1962.

KAHAN, Stanley. Introduction to Acting. Harcourt, Brace, and World, Inc., 1962.

Publications of The National Thespian Society, Cincinnati, Ohio.
    Selling Your Play by Richard S. Dunlop
    Staging Musicals by Robert W. Ensley
    Stage Lighting by Harold B. Obee
    Oral Interpretation by Leslie Irene Coger
    Make-Up for Stage and Television by Carl B. Cass
    Styles of Scenery Design by Williard J. Frederick
    Elements of Play Direction by Delwin B. Dusenbury
    High School Theatre by Robert W. Ensley
    Costumes Worn by Royalty by Charles R. Trumbo
    Period Furniture and Hand Props by Charles R. Trumbo
    From Fillets to Flappers by Charles R. Trumbo

PERIODICALS RECOMMENDED FOR READING

VARIETY A weekly commercial newspaper devoted solely to show business
One Year: $15.00 Two Years: $28.00 Three Years: $39.00
Variety Inc.
154 West 46th Street
New York, New York 10036

DRAMATICS The official organ of the National Thespian Society
One Year: $5.00 Single copy: $1.00
Dramatics
College Hill Station
Cincinnati, Ohio 45224

EDUCATIONAL THEATRE JOURNAL The official organ of the American Educational Theatre Association. It is sent to all members without charge quarterly, and is furnished on a subscription basis to libraries.
American Educational Theatre Association, Inc.
1701 Pennsylvania Avenue N.W.
Washington, D. C. 20006

THEATRE U S A
One Year: $3.00 Two Years: $5.00
Theatre U S A
Box 781
Elm Grove, Wisconsin 53122

SUNDAY EDITION OF NEW YORK TIMES
Six months: $15.70 One Year: $28.50
Subscription Manager
The New York Times
229 West 43rd Street
New York, New York 10036

PLAYS A commercial drama magazine for young people